KEN KESEY

MODERN LITERATURE SERIES

GENERAL EDITOR: Philip Winsor

In the same series:

S. Y. AGNON   *Harold Fisch*
SHERWOOD ANDERSON   *Welford Dunaway Taylor*
LEONID ANDREYEV   *Josephine M. Newcombe*
ISAAC BABEL   *R. W. Hallett*
JAMES BALDWIN   *Carolyn Wedin Sylvander*
SIMONE DE BEAUVOIR   *Robert Cottrell*
SAUL BELLOW   *Brigitte Scheer-Schäzler*
JORGE LUIS BORGES   *George R. McMurray*
BERTOLT BRECHT   *Willy Haas*
ANTHONY BURGESS   *Samuel Coale*
ALBERT CAMUS   *Carol Petersen*
TRUMAN CAPOTE   *Helen S. Garson*
WILLA CATHER   *Dorothy Tuck McFarland*
JOHN CHEEVER   *Samuel Coale*
COLETTE   *Robert Cottrell*
JOSEPH CONRAD   *Martin Tucker*
JULIO CORTÁZAR   *Evelyn Picon Garfield*
JOAN DIDION   *Katherine Usher Henderson*
JOHN DOS PASSOS   *George J. Becker*
THEODORE DREISER   *James Lundquist*
FRIEDRICH DÜRRENMATT   *Armin Arnold*
T. S. ELIOT   *Joachim Seyppel*
WILLIAM FAULKNER   *Joachim Seyppel*
F. SCOTT FITZGERALD   *Rose Adrienne Gallo*
FORD MADOX FORD   *Sondra J. Stang*
JOHN FOWLES   *Barry N. Olshen*
MAX FRISCH   *Carol Petersen*
ROBERT FROST   *Elaine Barry*
GABRIEL GÁRCIA MÁRQUEZ   *George R. McMurray*
MAKSIM GORKI   *Gerhard Habermann*
GÜNTER GRASS   *Kurt Lothar Tank*
ROBERT GRAVES   *Katherine Snipes*
PETER HANDKE   *Nicholas Hern*
LILLIAN HELLMAN   *Doris V. Falk*
ERNEST HEMINGWAY   *Samuel Shaw*
HERMANN HESSE   *Franz Baumer*
CHESTER HIMES   *James Lundquist*
HUGO VON HOFMANNSTHAL   *Lowell W. Bangerter*
CHRISTOPHER ISHERWOOD   *Claude J. Summers*
SARAH ORNE JEWETT   *Josephine Donovan*
UWE JOHNSON   *Mark Boulby*

(continued on last page of book)

KEN KESEY

Barry H. Leeds

FREDERICK UNGAR PUBLISHING CO.
NEW YORK

Library of Congress Cataloging in Publication Data

Leeds, Barry H.
    Ken Kesey.

    (Modern literature series)
    Bibliography: p.
    Includes index.
    1. Kesey, Ken—Criticism and interpretation.
I. Title.   II. Series: Modern literature monographs.
PS3561.E667Z75   813'.54   81-40466
ISBN 0-8044-2497-7   AACR2

*Once again to Robin
and to our children,
Brett Ashley and
Leslie Lion*

Contents

Acknowledgments

I am deeply grateful to Donna Miles for her cheerful and tireless work in typing the manuscript, and to Bob Miles and my wife, Robin, for their painstaking, intelligent reading of it. I wish to thank Central Connecticut State College for the sabbatical which enabled me to complete this book, and the CCSC Research Foundation for the grant which aided in manuscript preparation. Finally, I must record my gratitude to Anthony Piccione and David Flaherty for uncritical friendship, uncompromising support, and comic relief in times of stress.

Chronology

1935 Born in La Junta, Colorado, September 17.

1953 Graduates from high school.

1956 Marries Faye Haxby, May 20 (The Keseys now have four children: Shannon, Zane, Jed, and Sunshine).

1957 Receives B.A. from the University of Oregon at Eugene.

1958 Enters Stanford University creative writing program.

1960 Volunteers to be a subject for government experiments with "psychomimetic" drugs.

1962 Publishes *One Flew Over the Cuckoo's Nest* in February.

1963 Moves to La Honda, California. Dale Wasserman's stage adaptation of *Cuckoo's Nest*, starring Kirk Douglas, opens in New York, November 13.

1964 Publishes *Sometimes a Great Notion*. Takes cross-country bus trip with the Merry Pranksters.

1965 Arrested for possession of marijuana in April.

1966 Found guilty of drug charge in January. Arrested again while awaiting appeal. Becomes a fugitive in Mexico. Returns to United States in September. Arrested by FBI in October.

1967 Begins serving jail sentence. Released from jail in November; moves family to Pleasant Hill, Oregon.

1968 Tom Wolfe's *Electric Kool-Aid Acid Test* is published.

1969 Works for Apple in London. Revised version of Wasserman's *Cuckoo's Nest* opens in San Francisco.

1

Biography:
The Hallucinogenic
Outlaw

To a degree exceeded only by Norman Mailer and Ernest Hemingway, Ken Kesey has assumed a flamboyant public posture that has been bound to the critical and popular reception of his books. Although he has maintained a relatively low profile in recent years, Kesey achieved the personal notoriety of a cult hero during the 1960s, a fame which peaked with the 1968 publication of Tom Wolfe's pop biography, *The Electric Kool-Aid Acid Test*.[1] While Mailer's and Hemingway's public excesses have often obscured an understanding of their works, Kesey's sometimes lend a necessary dimension to reading his. The circumstances under which the novels were written often provide clues to the development of Kesey's technique, and the fleshing out of Kesey's thematic preoccupations in his life further illuminates his fictional vision.

Ken Elton Kesey was born on September 17, 1935, in La Junta, Colorado, the first of Fred and Geneva Smith Kesey's two sons. The family moved to Springfield, Oregon, where Kesey attended public schools and, despite a juvenile court appearance resulting from a prank at a local drive-in, was voted "most likely to succeed" upon graduation from high school. Although Kesey remembered his early childhood as "Low Rent," Fred Kesey became well-to-do after World War II by founding the Eugene Farmers

Cooperative and building it into a major dairy outlet.

Kesey graduated from the University of Oregon at Eugene, where he had been active in creative writing, drama, and sports. An outstanding wrestler in the 174-pound class, he later got as far as the 1960 Olympic eliminations in San Francisco. While in college, Kesey eloped with his high school sweetheart, Faye Haxby, on May 20, 1956. After graduation, he worked for a year, took some bit parts in Hollywood films, and completed an unpublished novel about college athletics entitled *End of Autumn*.

In 1958, Kesey entered Stanford University as a graduate student on a creative writing fellowship, studying with Malcolm Cowley and Wallace Stegner, among others. Living on Perry Lane, Stanford's bohemian quarter, he met Vik Lovell, a graduate student in psychology who introduced him to the two experiences which would precipitate the writing of *One Flew Over the Cuckoo's Nest*.[2] First, Lovell told him about experiments with "psychomimetic" drugs at the Veterans Hospital in Menlo Park. Volunteering as a paid subject, Kesey was introduced to numerous experimental drugs, some unpleasant in their effects, such as Ditran, and some which he enjoyed, notably LSD.

Kesey began to take LSD and other hallucinogens, especially peyote and mescaline, outside of the hospital. When Lovell suggested that he take a job as night attendant on the psychiatric ward at Menlo Park, the confluence of the two stimuli, the drugs and the hospital environment, led to the genesis of *Cuckoo's Nest*. Intrigued by the plight of the inmates, Kesey abandoned a novel he had been writing about San Francisco's North Beach, entitled *Zoo*, to begin one about a psychiatric ward. He often wrote under the influence of peyote, and according to Tom Wolfe, it was during such a session that the novel's narrator, Chief Broom, sprang into Kesey's mind:

For some reason peyote does this . . . Kesey starts getting

eyelid movies of faces . . . from out of nowhere. He knows
nothing about Indians and has never met an Indian, but suddenly here is a full-blown Indian—Chief Broom—the solu-
tion, the whole mothering key, to the novel. . . .[3]

This evaluation of the Chief's importance to the
novel's narrative and structural success is no exaggera-
tion. As will be emphasized in the critical discussion of
Cuckoo's Nest in Chapter 2, it is the Chief's highly subjective, hallucinatory first-person narrative that gives
the novel its metaphorical richness, its peculiar horror,
and its ultimate emotional force. By precipitating a
temporary mock-psychotic state in himself through the
use of psychomimetic drugs, Kesey was able to render
the novel credibly through the point of view of a
schizophrenic. A further instance of Kesey's intense
commitment to verisimilitude is that he arranged to be
given a clandestine electroshock therapy (EST) in
order to write about that experience.

After finishing *One Flew Over the Cuckoo's Nest*
in June 1961, Kesey moved his family back to Oregon,
first to Springfield and then to Florence, a logging
town near the ocean, where he began collecting material for *Sometimes a Great Notion*. The actual writing
of the second novel was done first on Perry Lane, and
after the leveling of Perry Lane by a developer in July
1963, on Kesey's newly acquired property in La
Honda, California. The critical and popular success
that immediately followed the February 1962 publication of *Cuckoo's Nest* provided Kesey with not only the
financial capital to buy the La Honda place but the
personal leverage to take over the moral and artistic
leadership of his old Perry Lane friends. To his entourage he added Neal Cassady—the model for Dean
Moriarty in Jack Kerouac's 1957 "Beat Generation"
novel, *On the Road*—and later, such diverse associates
as Beat poet Allen Ginsberg and the Hell's Angels.
Despite the absolute confidence which Kesey brought
to life at La Honda, seeking new mystical drug experiences and sweeping most of his friends along in the

wake of his enormous, engaging vitality, there were already those who began to become disaffected by his dominance, a preview of the incredible flights of egotism he was to take during the mid and late 1960s.

In the spring of 1964, after completing *Sometimes a Great Notion*, Kesey bought a 1939 International Harvester school bus. He and a band of friends calling themselves the Merry Pranksters painted it psychedelic colors, outfitted it with sophisticated taping and stereo equipment, stocked it with movie cameras, comic books, and assorted drugs, and set out on a cross-country trip to New York.

Tony Tanner says in *City of Words* that "The bus can be seen as Kesey's third novel."[4] Tom Wolfe indicates that after the publication of *Sometimes a Great Notion*, "Kesey was already talking about how writing was an old-fashioned and artificial form and pointing out, for all who cared to look . . . the bus."[5] The 1964 bus trip marked the point at which Kesey began to devote his energies primarily to shaping his own life and those of his satellites as an art form and a search for new perceptions. The publication in 1973 of the collection *Kesey's Garage Sale* would emphasize rather than disprove this commitment, in that *Garage Sale* is related more to a celebration of the values represented by the bus than to literary production as such, although Kesey did give indications in *Garage Sale* that he had begun to write seriously again.

The 1964 bus trip took Kesey and the Merry Pranksters across the southern states to New York and then back to La Honda via the northern route. En route, they shot more than forty hours of film, played pranks, and enjoyed confrontations with police, local citizens, Timothy Leary's League for Spiritual Discovery, and one another. Upon returning to La Honda, most of the group settled on Kesey's land, occupying themselves with cutting the film shot on the trip, which they referred to simply as "The Movie."

Tom Wolfe's treatment of the bus trip lends itself well to Tanner's conception of it as an elaborate fiction conceived and lived by Kesey. In *The Electric Kool-Aid Acid Test*, form is precisely suited to subject. Creating one of the best examples of the "nonfiction novel," Wolfe uses the novelistic techniques of characterization, dialogue, and undocumented reconstruction of hypothetical scenes. Most important, the structure of his work is novelistic in its use of flashback and selection of details. This selectivity enables Wolfe to render the tone of life aboard the bus without appearing to make any overt moral judgments. Nonetheless, the portrait which emerges is a horrific one, in which rivalries, defections, paranoia, and nervous breakdowns are rampant. The atmosphere inside the bus seems more often hysterical than merry, infernal rather than ecstatic.

Robert Scholes, reviewing *The Electric Kool-Aid Acid Test* in *Saturday Review*, incisively points out the primary strength of Wolfe's method:

He also has the double vision it takes to see Kesey as a genuine religious leader and a projection of a comic-book fantasy—both Buddha and Captain Marvel. Keeping his own cool, Wolfe ranges from strong empathy with Kesey's group to detached skepticism. This double perspective, simultaneously inside and outside the object of his investigation, is typical of his method.[6]

The reference to Captain Marvel is not idly chosen. Before either of his novels was written, Kesey already believed that the comic-book superheroes, "Superman, Captain Marvel . . . Captain America . . . The Flash," were the "honest American myths."[7] This notion was to influence Kesey's conception of Randle Patrick McMurphy in *One Flew Over the Cuckoo's Nest*, and to provide one of the primary symbol patterns in *Sometimes a Great Notion*. But its most dramatic reverberation during the period after 1964 lay in Kesey's perception of himself as a superhero.

Like all the Merry Pranksters, Kesey assumed a
nickname, "Swashbuckler."[8] Other Pranksters perceived him as "Dr. Strange,"[9] or even "The Incredible
Hulk."[10] Later, at a psychedelic event he called the
"Acid Test Graduation," Kesey would appear

bare chested, wearing only white leotards, a white satin cape
tied at the neck, and a red, white, and blue sash running
diagonally across his chest. It's . . . Captain America! The
Flash! Captain Marvel! the Superhero, in a word. . . .[11]

In his dominating presence, his affectation of
bizarre costumes, and his persistent and intrepid ex-
ploration of new frontiers of experience, Kesey
fashioned himself after the "honest American myths"
of the comic books. At the same time, in his drug-
abetted mysticism and almost sacramental administra-
tion of LSD to his followers, Kesey assumed the role of
religious leader to a growing cult. Meanwhile, his personal life continued to grow more bizarre.

In April 1965, Kesey was arrested for possession of
marijuana. In the ensuing year of appeals and court
appearances, the Pranksters continued and escalated
their manic escapades and use of hallucinogenic drugs.
During this period, Kesey engineered a strange and
short-lived alliance between the Hell's Angels and the
pacifistic hip subculture by opening his home to
representatives of both. With the link of Kesey's intense personality, and the ameliorating influence of
alcohol, marijuana, and LSD, a shaky but fascinating
juxtaposition of cultures was effected. A man of
physical prowess and intellect, "Kesey was the magnet
and the strength, the man in both worlds."[12]

The pressure of his impending trial had taken its
toll on Kesey, who

looked like he had aged ten years in three months. . . . He
was taking a lot of speed and smoking a lot of grass. He
looked haggard. . . . Kesey was doing some acid rapping,
taking 500, 1000, 1,500 micrograms instead of the normal
100 to 250. He had always been against that.[13]

During at least one such trip, Kesey arrived at the drug-induced illusion that he was God, that he had "all the power in the world,"[14] a situation that he would later deal with in his screenplay, "Over the Border," in *Kesey's Garage Sale*.

Kesey's mental state was such at this point that when he was invited to speak at an antiwar rally in Berkeley by the Vietnam Day Committee, he rambled on so disjointedly and antagonistically that he alienated the audience. In league with Owsley—Augustus Owsley Stanley III, the LSD manufacturer, fabled "White Rabbit" of the subculture, and founder of the Grateful Dead rock group—Kesey arranged several public "acid tests" at which LSD was distributed free to all, and thus completed his alienation from such relatively respectable LSD advocates as Richard Alpert, who, with Timothy Leary, had sacrificed his academic career for his belief in psychedelic drugs.

Therefore, Kesey was already cut off not merely from the mainstream, establishment society he had rejected but from many erstwhile allies and friends as well when he became, literally, an outlaw and a fugitive. On January 17, 1966, a judge found Kesey guilty of the April 1965 charge of possession of narcotics. Two days later, while awaiting appeal, he was again arrested for possession, this time in the company of the nineteen-year-old Mountain Girl (Carolyn Adams), one of the closest members of his entourage, who was later to bear Kesey's fourth child, Sunshine. Facing a probable five-year jail sentence, Kesey fled to Mexico and remained a fugitive for the better part of 1966.

In 1959, Norman Mailer coined the term "psychic outlaw." Writing of his reaction to a shabby betrayal by a publisher, he concluded:

I finally had the simple sense to understand that if I wanted my work to travel further than others, the life of my talent depended on fighting a little more and looking for help a little less. . . . All I felt was that I was an outlaw, a psychic outlaw, and I liked it, I liked it a good night better than trying to be a gentleman. . . .[15]

The term "psychic outlaw" lends itself to many protagonists in contemporary fiction, from Salinger's Holden Caulfield to Donleavy's Sebastian Dangerfield to Mailer's Stephen Rojack. Increasingly, the focus of the American novel since World War II has been upon protagonists who accept or seek a role outside society. In American or British novels of previous eras, even so roguish a character as Henry Fielding's Tom Jones, living on the periphery of his society, could ultimately find a place within that society in the resolution of the novel. Today, a gathering disaffection with our society's hypocrisies renders such resolutions less attractive. Certainly, such is the case in Kesey's work.

Like Mailer, Kesey has developed the philosophy of the outlaw in both his fiction and his life. In *Cuckoo's Nest* and *Sometimes a Great Notion*, McMurphy and Hank Stamper choose to oppose the strictures of the regimented society which attempts to hem them in. Kesey, in an equally dramatic manner, embraced the role of outlaw himself. On the eve of his flight to Mexico, he said, "If society wants me to be an outlaw . . . then I'll be an outlaw, and a damned good one. That's something people need. People at all times need outlaws."[16] Later, at the nadir of his period of exile in Mexico, Kesey reminded himself that a "man should move off his sure center out onto the outer edges, that the outlaw, even more than the artist, is he who tests the limits of life. . . ."[17]

Kesey's nine-month flight to avoid prosecution was a comedy of errors. A suicide note intended as a diversionary tactic was treated as a prank by the police. Word of his exile in Puerto Vallarta leaked, and he fled in disguise to Mazatlan, where he was joined by Faye, their children, the pregnant Mountain

Girl, and other Pranksters. (After marrying Prankster George Walker in order to ensure the child's legal rights under Mexican law, Mountain Girl gave birth to her daughter, Sunshine, who now lives with the Keseys.)

After several close calls, notably an episode in which he escaped from Mexican Federales by jumping aboard a passing freight train, Kesey secretly reentered the United States in late September 1966, posing as a drunken cowboy singer riding a horse. Back in California, he taunted law enforcement authorities by making surprise public appearances and granting clandestine newspaper and television interviews. In one of these, for the San Francisco *Chronicle*, he said, "I intend to stay in this country as a fugitive and as salt in J. Edgar Hoover's wounds."[18] In October, he was captured on a freeway and arrested by the FBI.

After two trials ended in hung juries, Kesey pleaded *nolo contendere* to a lesser charge ("knowingly being in a place where marijuana was kept"), dropped his appeal for the original charge of possession, and in June 1967 began to serve both sentences concurrently, first at the San Mateo County Jail and then at the San Mateo County Sheriff's Honor Camp. Released in November 1967, he moved with his family to Pleasant Hill, Oregon, where he still lives and raises dairy cattle.

Between 1968 and 1973, Kesey lived in relative seclusion. He wrote and drew an expanded version of his jail journals, entitled *Cut the Mother-Fuckers Loose*, which he has said may eventually be the basis of a novel. He published short pieces and letters in underground magazines, and he gave several interviews. During 1969, Kesey worked for Apple in London for three months; and in 1971, he co-edited *The Last Supplement to the Whole Earth Catalogue* with Paul Krassner.

In 1973, *Kesey's Garage Sale* was published, bringing new Kesey work to a large reading audience for the first time since the publication of *Sometimes a Great Notion* in 1964. The book is a potpourri of letters, interviews, previously published occasional pieces, and contributions by such friends as Ken Babbs, Neal Cassady, and Allen Ginsberg, with an introduction by Arthur Miller. It is useful in monitoring Kesey's progress in and attitudes toward his career as a writer of fiction.

The most important piece in *Garage Sale* is Kesey's screenplay "Over the Border," which makes up more than half the volume. The screenplay is a fictionalized, even surrealistic account of Kesey's adventures and misadventures as a fugitive in Mexico. If other sections of *Garage Sale* illuminate his past work or suggest possibilities for his future as a novelist, "Over the Border" connects the two, providing a look backward and ahead in terms of Kesey's life as well as his work. In its conclusion, Kesey recognizes and repudiates the egotism and selfishness of his attitudes and actions during the mid-1960s and implicitly announces a new personal and artistic maturity.

Since 1973, Kesey has grown gradually more visible and prolific. In October 1974, he traveled to Egypt for *Rolling Stone* to write a five-part series of articles entitled "The Search for the Secret Pyramid." In an abortive and celebrated episode, he worked on the screenplay for the 1975 movie version of *One Flew Over the Cuckoo's Nest* until bitter disagreements with the producers caused the association to be terminated amid threats of legal repercussions from Kesey.[19] I will deal with the relative merits and weaknesses of the movie version as well as those of Dale Wasserman's stage adaptation of *Cuckoo's Nest* in a later chapter.

In the March 1976 issue of *Esquire*, Kesey published a semiautobiographical piece entitled "Abdul and Ebenezer," dealing with life on a dairy farm, which will be part of a projected collection entitled *The Demon Box*. In the same month, he allowed himself and his family to be featured in a *People* magazine "Bio."[20]

In *Garage Sale*, Kesey and his friends announced their intention to publish, under the auspices of Intrepid Trips Information Service, a little magazine entitled *Spit in the Ocean* (SITO), to be released irregularly for a total of seven issues. To date, five issues have appeared. In addition to his editorial work throughout the publication run of SITO, Kesey has contributed such pieces as the apparently autobiographical memoir "The Thrice-thrown Tranny Man" in the first issue and the reprint of "Search for the Secret Pyramid" in the fifth. But the most interesting aspect of SITO is that Kesey has been writing a seven-part serialized novel entitled *Seven Prayers by Grandma Whittier* for the magazine. It is expected that this will be Kesey's next published novel.

A final observation is in order. The protagonist of "Over the Border," the first-person narrator of "Abdul and Ebenezer" and "The Thrice-thrown Tranny Man," and Grandma Whittier's "famous" grandson in *Seven Prayers* is a recurrent character named Devlin Deboree, who closely resembles Kesey. In fact, when Kesey reprinted "Search for the Secret Pyramid" in SITO, one of the few editorial changes he made was to substitute "Devlin Deboree" for his own name in the few places where it had appeared in the *Rolling Stone* version. In every case, Deboree's wife is named Betsy, his children Caleb, Quiston, and Sherree. In all the Devlin Deboree pieces, whether they are factual, fictional, or an amalgam of the two genres, readily identifiable autobiographical details abound, particularly in "Tranny Man" and "Abdul and Ebenezer."

This device is intriguing. It may be largely a puckish whim, similar to Alfred Hitchcock's brief, unobtrusive appearance in each of his films. Yet Devlin

Deboree's appearances are not always unobtrusive; and despite the demonstrated hazards of biographical criticism, despite the difficulty of making clear judgments on Kesey's recent writings in their present fragmented state, despite the fact that *Seven Prayers* appears to be taking shape as a work of pure imagination, I cannot resist seeing the Deboree syndrome as symptomatic of the degree to which Kesey's art continues to be profoundly touched by his own forceful personality.

2

One Flew Over
the Cuckoo's Nest:
"It's True Even
If It Didn't Happen"

Kesey's first novel, *One Flew Over the Cuckoo's Nest*, has been enormously popular at every level of academe for almost two decades. It is a book which holds the interest of the undergraduate who can say, "I'm not *into* reading." Yet its accessibility is deceptive; it is by no means a simple book. Close critical analysis illuminates the depth of Kesey's technical mastery of such aspects of novelistic form as symbolism and structure.

If these are essentially academic concerns, the success with which technique serves theme in this work is not. A careful reading of several central symbol patterns and an understanding of the narrative devices used to present them both enhance an appreciation of Kesey's art and show clearly that the central thematic thrust of this novel strikes even closer to the heart of the American experience now than it did in 1962.

Within a highly disciplined form, Kesey has dealt with issues which loom prominently in the minds of those whose primary criterion for any idea or pursuit is its "relevance." The questioning of a monolithic bureaucratic order, the rejection of stereotyped sexual roles, the simultaneous awareness that healthy sexuality and a clear sense of sexual identity are prerequisites for human emotional survival, the recognition and rejection of hypocrisy, the devotion to the expression of individual identity: all these leap into sharp focus through a study of Kesey's technique.

Randle Patrick McMurphy, the protagonist of *One Flew Over the Cuckoo's Nest*, is a man who has consistently resisted the strictures of society. Having decided that life on a psychiatric ward will be preferable to hard labor on the county work farm where he has been serving a sentence for assault and battery, McMurphy feigns insanity. This brings him into dramatic confrontation with "Big Nurse," a representative of the most repressive aspects of American society. Big Nurse is backed by the power of a mechanistic "Combine," a central agency for that society's suppression of individuality.

During his stay on her ward, McMurphy fights a constant guerrilla action against Big Nurse and her aides. He rallies the other patients behind him as he introduces gambling, laughter, and human vitality to the ward. He leads the patients on a therapeutically rejuvenating deep-sea fishing trip. In a penultimate rebellion, he smuggles whores and liquor onto the ward for a hilarious party.

Against this humorous backdrop, the struggle between McMurphy and Big Nurse continues to escalate. In the climactic final scenes, she is able to provoke him into outbursts of violence which provide the excuse to "treat" McMurphy with electro shock therapy (EST) and ultimately with a lobotomy. In the moving conclusion, McMurphy's friend Chief Bromden mercifully smothers him to death and makes his own escape. Although McMurphy is ultimately destroyed, he is not defeated. His courage and humor are never broken. Even after his death, his spirit pervades the ward; it is clear that he has beaten Big Nurse and damaged the Combine.

It is not only McMurphy's own struggle which is

at issue in this novel. For one thing, McMurphy comes to represent the only hope for salvation open to his fellow inmates, a salvation which he brings about through the tutelage of example, making them aware of their own manhood in the dual senses of masculinity and humanity. Also, the novel's first-person narrator, Chief Bromden, assumes during the course of the novel a rebel role similar to that of McMurphy.

In a narrative structure analogous to that employed by F. Scott Fitzgerald in *The Great Gatsby*,[1] Kesey places Chief Bromden in a pivotal position. In both novels, the narrator is a man closely associated with the protagonist and torn by ambivalent feelings of disapproval and admiration for him, who, during the course of the novel, learns and develops through the tutelary example of the protagonist's life and ultimate death, and who, in recounting the story of his friend's life, clarifies his own development to the point where he takes on both the strengths of the protagonist and an awareness of how to avoid a similar downfall and death. Bromden and Nick Carraway both become syntheses of their own latent strengths and abilities and the best aspects of McMurphy and Gatsby. This narrative structure provides the novelist with the advantages of both the first-person point of view (within which the narrator can be revealed in terms of his own internal cerebration) and a third-person (hence more credibly objective) view of the novel's central figure.

The progressive development of the characters of McMurphy and Bromden cannot be said to parallel one another; a more accurate geometric metaphor is that of two intersecting oblique lines: As McMurphy's strength wanes, Bromden moves toward the ascendant. But the two developments proceed simultaneously and are integral to one another, until the transfer of power from McMurphy to Bromden is complete.

Bromden is an American Indian, a 280-pound,

6 foot 8 inch former high school football player and combat veteran of World War II who has been robbed of identity and sanity by the combination of pressures brought to bear on him by twentieth-century American society. At the outset of the novel, he is literally cut off from even the most rudimentary communication. He is so fearful of the dangers of dealing with people that he has learned to feign total deafness and has maintained absolute silence for years. Considered incurable by the medical staff, he is forced to perform menial janitorial work by the orderlies, who ridicule him with the title "Chief Broom."

The nickname has an obvious significance: Defined by his menial function, Bromden is no more than an object to the staff, a tool. But even his legal name, "Bromden," represents a false identity that is imposed upon him by others. Ironically, Chief Broom really is the son of a tribal chief, a once-powerful leader whose Indian name meant "The-Pine-That-Stands-Tallest-on-the-Mountain." "Bromden" is the maiden name of his mother, a white woman; and the fact that his father allowed himself to be henpecked into adopting it is invested with great significance by Kesey. The loss of pride in the Indian heritage brought about by the pressure of white American society (especially its matriarchal element, as represented by Mrs. Bromden) lies at the heart of the twentieth-century problem of Bromden, his father, and their people. The plight of the American Indian comes to represent, for Kesey, that of the American individualist in highly distilled form. The artificial identities of "Mr. Bromden" and "Chief Broom" imposed upon Bromden by the matriarchal and mechanistic elements of society diminish him enormously. The first robs him of his masculine pride and his racial identity, the second of his very humanity. Kesey forces us to abstract from this extreme case the realization that our own identities as self-determining individuals have been considerably eroded and are further threatened by a computerized civilization.

The experiences which have undermined Bromden's strength and sanity are revealed later in the novel in brief flashbacks, each precipitated by McMurphy as he persists in forcing Bromden to leave his fortress of silence and forgetfulness and reenter by stages the external world. As McMurphy makes friendly overtures toward him, Bromden begins to remember and understand episodes from his own past. In persistently attempting communication with Bromden, McMurphy functions as a sort of combination lay psychiatrist and confessor, precipitating more and more painful and traumatic memories out of Bromden's mind until the Chief is able to face his own problems and begin the trip back to manhood.

These flashbacks help establish for the reader an acceptance of Bromden as a sympathetic and fully developed character of considerable potential so that his later resurgence of power is both credible and emotionally charged. In addition, these passages are thematically useful to the author, introducing graphic substantiation of his central indictment of the Combine-controlled American society and its capacity to crush individuality and communication. Chief Broom is the tangible representation of the human alienation produced by the system.

A good example of the use Kesey makes of Bromden's memories is the passage in which Bromden recounts his traumatic, dehumanizing experiences in combat on Anzio. The placement of Bromden's flashbacks is so effectively controlled that they become an example and a bulwark of the tight control of plot structure by which Kesey develops his theme. Kesey is able to observe a set of personal limitations similar to the classical unities, limiting his "onstage" action to a small immediate area and a relatively short time while substantiating character and theme by introducing each flashback at the most dramatically effective point in the narrative.

What is particularly impressive about *One Flew Over the Cuckoo's Nest* as a first novel is the highly credible integration of prose style and metaphorical patterns with the character of Bromden. Early in the book, Bromden's perceptions and the very rhythms of his speech are both informed and limited by his disturbed mental state. As he moves toward sanity and effective communication with others, Bromden perceives and articulates more clearly, and the prose style of the narrative reflects this development precisely. For example, fairly late in the novel, Bromden, who has been subject to frequent hallucination, takes the significant step of drawing a clear distinction between illusion and reality:

There was little brown birds occasionally on the fence; when a puff of leaves would hit the fence the birds would fly off with the wind. It looked at first like the leaves were hitting the fence and turning into birds and flying away.

Bromden's hallucinations during the earlier part of the novel serve to establish and support the central aesthetic of the book, based on a fascinating subjectivity within which Kesey masterfully commands a suspension of disbelief. This is brought about largely through absolute candor on Bromden's part. He admits his own subjectivity and the extent of his alienation from our societal "reality," but in a crucial statement which sums up precisely the relationship between the rich metaphorical structure of his hallucinations and the central truths they elucidate, Bromden tells us (referring to the entire McMurphy story): "It's true even if it didn't happen." It is the absence of this distinctive hallucinatory perspective that most weakens the movie version of *Cuckoo's Nest*.

Thus, the truths Bromden forces us to recognize are not dependent for their validity upon drawing a

distinction between which of the events he recounts
"really" happened and which proceed entirely out of
his own labyrinthine imagination. When, for example, Bromden crushes a tranquilizer capsule and sees
(in the split second before it self-destructs upon contact
with the air and turns to white powder) that it is a
miniature electronic element, intended by the Combine to control the man who swallows it, it is not
necessary for the reader to determine what is illusion
and what is "reality." The truth lies in the metaphor of
the hallucination: The capsule, no matter what its
ostensibly beneficial effect, is a device intended by
society to control the inmates, to render them docile
and bovine, and to rob them of any individual trait
which might threaten the homogeneity and mediocrity
of the established order.

   Each of Bromden's hallucinations forms part of a
complex system of recurrent symbols, and each is
ultimately shown by Kesey to grow naturally out of
Bromden's previous experiences. The transistor
metaphor becomes part of a more comprehensive
theory of Bromden's that the Combine exerts direct
control over the citizenry through electronic devices;
thus the reader is not surprised when Bromden later
remarks in passing that he has studied electronics in
the army and in his one year of college. When old Pete
Bancini, a man so mentally retarded that the Combine
has been unable to exercise control over him, physically resists the orderlies' efforts to subdue him, the
hallucination Bromden creates of Pete's fist pumping
up into the form of a huge steel ball ties into a
recurrent series of references to hands as symbols of
potency.

   The psychological verisimilitude employed by
Kesey in establishing these image patterns as natural
outgrowths of Bromden's experience is so painstak-
ingly precise that even the briefest metaphors used by
Bromden can be traced to their source. For example,

one morning Bromden is served a "canned peach on a piece of green, torn lettuce." Later, relating the story of how the orderlies forcibly administered medication to an inmate, Bromden describes the scene in the same terms: "One sits on his head and the other rips his pants open in back and peels the cloth until Taber's peach-colored rear is framed by the ragged lettuce-green."

Perhaps the most frightening product of Bromden's hallucinatory perception is the Combine itself. He defines it as a "huge organization that aims to adjust the Outside as well as the Big Nurse has the Inside." The Inside, as Bromden sees it, is different from the outside world only in the *degree* of control which must be exerted over its inhabitants. The Combine, committed as it is to the supremacy of technology over humanity, extends its influence by dehumanizing men and making them machines. But as the novel progresses, it becomes clear that Kesey envisions emasculation as a preliminary step in the dehumanization process. Ultimately, a pattern emerges: The Combine functions on two levels, mechanistic and matriarchal. The two are fused in the Big Nurse, Miss Ratched, who is a "high ranking official" of the Combine.

Big Nurse herself is conceived in mechanistic terms. Even her name, "Ratched," sounds like a kind of wrench or machine component, and the association with "rat" makes its very sound unpleasant. Bromden sees her as an expensive piece of precision-made machinery, marred in its functional design only by a pair of oversized breasts. Despite her annoyance at being forced to carry them, and despite Bromden's feeling that they mark an obvious flaw in an otherwise perfect piece of work, their presence is not inconsistent with the symbolic irony intended by Kesey. Miss Ratched's breasts are ironic reminders of the sexuality she has renounced. At the novel's end, they will be exposed by McMurphy as the palpable symbol of her vulnerability. Finally, they are her badge of membership in the Smothering Mother cadre of the Combine.

Nurse Ratched is frequently referred to, in varying degrees of admiration or irony, by the hospital's public relations man and by the inmates themselves as the "mother" of the men on her ward. As Kesey presents it, the role is an evil one. The problems of many of the men on the ward are largely sexual in origin, and in a number of cases an overbearing mother has contributed largely to the problem. Big Nurse, under the guise of compassion, perpetuates, through the role of solicitous mother, the debilitating environment which already has emasculated the inmates.

Upon McMurphy's arrival at the ward, he tells the inmates that "the court ruled that I'm a psychopath. . . . Now they tell me a psychopath's a guy that fights too much and fucks too much. . . ." Although Kesey renders McMurphy's character in such a way that his sanity never seems questionable to the reader, it is significant that his cunning but unschooled ruse is so readily acceptable both to prison authorities and to the medical staff of the hospital. The central issue seems to be that the two areas in which McMurphy's animal vitality manifests itself, rage and sexual energy, form a two-pronged threat to the dual repressive roles of the Combine: mechanistic order and matriarchal emasculation. Having classified brawling and promiscuous sexual activity as "antisocial" forms of behavior, the authorities make the easy assumption that a man who sees such behavior as a desirable and valid form of life must be insane.

McMurphy, for his part, recognizes Big Nurse's methods almost immediately:

What she is is a ball-cutter. I've seen a thousand of 'em, old and young, men and women . . . people who try to make you weak so they can get you to . . . live like they want you to. . . . If you're up against a guy who wants to win by making you weaker instead of making himself stronger, then watch for his knee . . . that's what that old buzzard is doing. . . .

This distinction between winning by making one's opponent weaker as opposed to making oneself stronger is central to McMurphy's ethic. A recurrent thematic concern of Kesey's, it prefigures the conflict between Lee and Hank Stamper in *Sometimes a Great Notion*.

The conflict which Bromden perceives between the individual and the Combine has in his experience never been a true contest. The Combine and, by extension, Big Nurse, appear monolithic and invincible to Bromden. Nurse Ratched's power derives largely from the apparatus of a society concerned with the maintenance of harmonious mediocrity: locked doors, psychiatric jargon, Seconal, EST. But it is also based in large part on human elements within her control. At her bidding, the patients spy on each other, ostensibly for therapeutic reasons. She has, over a period of years, created a constant turnover of doctors before finding Dr. Spivey, a man weak enough to be manipulated. In much the same way, she has gone through an enormous number of black orderlies on a trial basis, dismissing scores of them before finding those who are so full of hatred that they will zealously fulfill the task of subduing and humiliating the inmates. Foremost among their methods is the habit of brutal homosexual rape. The hatred and violence by which the act is characterized serve both to dehumanize the aides themselves and to underscore the emasculation of the inmates, removing the last vestige of their pride and reducing them to *objects* of humiliation.

The fact that the process of selection for both aides and doctors has taken some years makes it clear that Kesey is not making simplistic judgments against particular racial or occupational groups. In conjunction with the plight of Chief Bromden, the black aides' rage against white people is shown to be a *result* of racism, and thus Kesey makes an indictment against racial prejudice as a self-perpetuating process. In addition, the novel is strewn with sympathetic exceptions to these characters. Mr. Turkle, the black night orderly, is an attractive character, who abets and participates in the patients' clandestine party. The Japanese nurse in charge of the Disturbed Ward repudiates Nurse Ratched's methods. Dr. Spivey, by the novel's conclusion, begins to assert himself. Even the use of EST as a punitive measure is carefully shown to be atypical, peculiar to Big Nurse's ward.

From the outset, McMurphy pays more attention to Bromden than anyone has in years. Where others have belittled the Chief, McMurphy marvels at his size and recognizes the latent strength it represents. Almost immediately, McMurphy begins to establish contact with Bromden, although it is at first superficial and unarticulated. In a passage which significantly prefigures the central thematic process of the book, the transfusion of power from McMurphy to Bromden, McMurphy offers to shake hands with Bromden, who, unwilling to relinquish the protection of his feigned deafness, remains passive and stares dumbly at the outstretched hand. McMurphy picks up Bromden's limp hand, with the result that "my hand commenced to feel peculiar and went to swelling up out there on my stick of an arm, like he was transmitting his own blood into it. It rang with blood and power. It blowed up near as big as his, I remember." The pumping up of Bromden's hand is an erectile image, parallel to that of Old Pete in the steel ball hallucination, which progresses to an explicit genital reference later in the book, when Bromden experiences his first erection in years. The pattern is repeated throughout the novel, with hands as a symbol of male potency introducing the more crucial issue of emasculation.

McMurphy's hands are of primary importance.

Immediately before McMurphy shakes Bromden's hand, the Chief is impressed enough to give the reader a lengthy description of McMurphy's offered hand. It is a record of his tough, nomadic life, with various scars, tattoos, and stains detailing the occupations, struggles, and general life-style of the man. Bromden concludes, "The palm was callused, and the calluses were cracked, and dirt was worked in the cracks. A road map of his travels up and down the West." Not only is this hand a map of the land which Bromden will later find his way back to; it quite literally carries in its cracks some of the earth from that land.

The experience and power which repose in McMurphy's hands are emphasized repeatedly. Later, during the fishing trip, he is able to intimidate two surly service station attendants without striking a blow by showing them his calluses and scars.

The symbolic value of hands is important in other characters as well, notably Dale Harding, a slender, sensitive, almost effeminate man who has retreated behind a shield of intellectual irony because he feels unable to cope with his big-breasted, sexually demanding wife. Harding's hands are an index of his character: "hands so long and white and dainty I think they carved each other out of soap . . . it bothers him that he's got pretty hands." Harding's feeling of shame at his "pretty" hands is reinforced when his wife, on her visit to the hospital, derides the male friends who have visited their home in his absence for their "limp wrists." More obviously and crucially, when the World Series vote approaches, McMurphy prods Harding by asking,

"You afraid if you raise your hand that old Buzzard'll cut it off."

Harding lifts one thin eyebrow. "Perhaps I am; perhaps I *am* afraid she'll cut it off if I raise it."

Harding is too intelligent a man not to be aware of the

dual significance of his own statement; and the admitted fear of symbolic castration ties into another obvious manifestation of the theme of sexual identity. All the men have been to one degree or another emasculated; but the horror of the situation is dramatically underlined by a literal castration, when an inmate commits suicide by amputation: "Old Rawler. Cut both nuts off and bled to death, sitting right on the can in the latrine. . . ."

It should be made clear that the polarity established between the externally effeminate hands of Harding and the more obviously masculine hands of McMurphy is not a simplistic one. Although Harding's "pretty" hands are a symbolic manifestation of his confused sexual identity, it is Harding himself who sees them as shameful, not McMurphy or Bromden. The brand of manhood admired by Kesey and represented by McMurphy is not limited exclusively to brawny men with scarred hands, as is shown by the fact that Harding grows to manhood by the novel's end under McMurphy's tutelage without changing his physical appearance and by Bromden's revelation that McMurphy is no stereotyped beer advertisement he-man:

I'd see him do things that didn't fit with his face or hands, things like painting a picture at OT with real paints on a blank paper with no lines or numbers . . . or like writing letters to someone in a beautiful flowing hand. . . . He hadn't let what he looked like run his life. . . .

Being a man is more than being physically strong or even courageous. It entails sensitivity and a commitment to other people, because manhood, as Kesey sees it, is not merely the quality of being male but of being human. What McMurphy teaches the inmates is not merely how to be aware and proud of their sexual identity but how to be human beings as well, responsible for one another. In the process, he himself develops greater maturity and responsibility, progressing from good-natured selfishness to a selfless commitment to his fellows.

As McMurphy's determination and influence increase, the threat posed by his sexual vitality is so clear that even the most superficial accoutrements which attach to him—the sound of laughter and song, the smell of sweat—are condemned by Big Nurse as disruptive and "dirty." Ultimately, the issue is that McMurphy is opposed to sterility in both its medical and symbolic implications. What makes this opposition particularly effective is that he is not susceptible to the Combine's most insidious weapon, guilt. When Miss Ratched assigns McMurphy the job of cleaning toilet bowls, he turns the menial task into a humiliation for her rather than for himself, writing an obscene word backward inside the rim of one bowl so that when she inspects it with a hand mirror she is startled. She tells McMurphy that his job is to make the place cleaner, not dirtier. The humor of the incident does not detract from the serious thematic implication, the polarity between the mechanical sterility of Big Nurse and the fertile animality of McMurphy.

The barrier between the two is a tangible as well as a symbolic one: the glass shield which surrounds the nurses' station, separating Big Nurse from the men but allowing her to spy on them. McMurphy calls the enclosed office a "Hothouse," an intuitive metaphor which strikes at the heart of the issue, for the office is the center of a sterile environment which makes the inmates dependent and thus unable to survive in the outside world. One of the crucial events of the book is McMurphy's breaking of this barrier by deliberately running his *hand* through it. The breaking of the protective barrier, Big Nurse's horror, the presence of blood, and the recurrence of the hand as symbol emphasize the sexual implications of the act as well as the movement from sterility to fertility represented throughout by McMurphy.

Big Nurse has a number of allies and subordinate satellites, notably the supervisor of the hospital, another old army nurse who is a lifelong friend of Miss Ratched. A second friend and ally is the hospital receptionist, mother of Billy Bibbit. Billy is a particularly sympathetic character who, under the double load of two mothers, his own and Miss Ratched, is ultimately broken. On the other extreme of the female hierarchy is Candy, a whore friend of McMurphy who is feminine in a most attractive way. She likes men, enjoys sex, and ultimately holds out the only hope Billy Bibbit has ever had of becoming a man. Associated with Candy are several similar women, including her companion Sandy and the sexually open women who come alive in McMurphy's tales of his past.

The clearest example of the American woman caught indecisively in the untenable position between these two extremes is Vera Harding, Dale's wife. Like Nurse Ratched, she is big-breasted and garishly disguised by cosmetics, and like Ratched, she has subtly contributed to the erosion of her husband's masculinity. Nonetheless, Vera Harding still possesses the potential to move toward the camp of Candy, as Kesey shows in a scene in which she meets and flirts with McMurphy. Although Vera uses her sexuality as a weapon of subjugation, she is at least aware and proud of it. In her conversation with McMurphy, Vera reveals herself as a person who moves instinctively in search of a viable heterosexual relationship; despite her dubious methods and her own lack of perception about her plight, her harsh qualities are mitigated somewhat. Although Vera has damaged her husband's sense of sexual identity, he has failed her in similar fashion by abdicating too readily the responsibilities of the male role. It is one measure of the qualified hope Kesey offers for future male-female relations in America that by the novel's end Dale Harding is able to accept some of this responsibility and sign himself out of the hospital to try again, armed with a new honesty derived from his contact with McMurphy.

Those inmates who are totally irreclaimable by society for use as tools are, significantly, termed "vegetables." But there are intermediate steps in the dehumanizing process; and in their regressive develop- ment toward their ultimate roles as machines or vegetables, the patients, brutalized by Big Nurse and her orderlies, are pointedly and repeatedly compared by Kesey to various animals: a dog, a bug, a gorilla, a mare, a moose, and a mustang, among others.

In addition, several extended patterns of animal imagery are employed by Kesey. Early in the book, Harding expresses to McMurphy his own metaphor for the situation in the ward. He sees himself and his fellow inmates as rabbits incapable of surviving without the repressive supervision of a wolf such as Miss Ratched. He suggests that McMurphy too may be a wolf. Although McMurphy rejects Harding's metaphor, annoyed that the patients can consider themselves anything but men, he has already ventured an analogy of his own, describing the first group therapy meeting he attends as a "bunch of chickens at a peckin' party."

Other bird images occur as well. When Bromden first attempts to laugh, he sounds "like a pullet trying to crow." Miss Ratched is often compared to a buz- zard. The novel's title makes use of a slang connotation of "cuckoo." But the image pattern which is set in direct opposition to the pejorative connotations of the chicken simile is that which attaches to the wild goose. Although early references to the goose are humorous and deprecating (McMurphy and Harding argue over the dubious honor of who is to be the "bull goose loony," and later Harding evaluates McMurphy's sen- sitivity as no more than that of a goose), this bird comes to represent the pride and self-determination to which men should aspire. When, on his way to

recovery, Bromden looks out of the dormitory window
at night, viewing the outside world clearly for the first
time in many years, he sees a young dog excitedly ex-
ploring for new experiences. Then, both Bromden and
the dog are entranced by the majestic passage of a
flock of Canada honkers:

I heard a high, laughing gabble. . . . Then they crossed the
moon—a black, weaving necklace, drawn into a V by that
lead goose. For an instant that lead goose was right in the
center of that circle, bigger than the others, a black cross
opening and closing. . . .

This passage suggests an interpretation of the novel's
title. McMurphy, "bigger than the others," wild and
free and migratory, is like the lead goose, pulling his
followers in the direction he has chosen. Never truly
trapped and grounded by the ward's restrictions,
McMurphy does fly over the "cuckoo's nest." In fact,
upon his first admission to the ward, McMurphy
"sounds like he's . . . sailing fifty yards overhead,
hollering at those below on the ground. He sounds
big." In addition, the "laughing" sound of the geese's
gabble and the metaphor of the cross echo patterns
which attach to McMurphy, as does the fact that in the
center of the moon's circle the lead goose wears a sort
of halo.

If at this point the goose symbolism attaches
primarily to McMurphy, the young dog is associated
with Bromden. In the episode quoted above, both
Bromden and the dog experience the awakening of
new sensations. During his escape, Bromden runs "in
the direction I remember seeing the dog go." The symbol cluster of goose and dog is, however, a complex
one, in which Bromden is ultimately associated with
the goose and McMurphy with the dog. Insofar as he
grows "bigger," takes over McMurphy's leadership
role, and ultimately flies from the "cuckoo's nest"—"I
felt like I was flying. Free."—Bromden assumes the

strengths of the Canada honker. His ultimate destination is Canada.

Perhaps the most poignant aspect of this pattern is the foreshadowing of McMurphy's fate by that of the dog. The last glimpse Bromden has of the dog, before he is pulled from the window by the night nurse, Miss Pilbow, shows the animal heading toward the highway, "loping steady and solemn like he had an appointment." A car comes out of a turn, and Bromden sees the "dog and the car making for the same spot of pavement." Later, when McMurphy is about to make the difficult decision to escalate his rebellion against Big Nurse, he is compared to a dog overcoming his fear of a dangerous adversary; and just before McMurphy announces his decision by breaking the window of the nurses' station, Bromden hears a sound in his head "like tires speeding down a pavement." The implicit parallel is clear: McMurphy and the dog, vital and vulnerable, move inexorably toward their head-on collisions with massive machines—the Combine and the car.

The credibility of McMurphy's character stems largely from the fact that several times in the escalating struggle with Big Nurse he falters, backing off before taking the painful step to the next plateau of courage and commitment. Bromden's growing personal involvement in McMurphy's battle is emphasized by the fact that his narration is clearly influenced in tone and content by McMurphy's behavior. When McMurphy succeeds in a particularly absurd practical joke at Big Nurse's expense, Bromden recalls similar situations perpetrated upon white bureaucrats by his father and other tribesmen, in the happier time before Pine-That-Stands-Tallest-on-the-Mountain was beaten by Mrs. Bromden and the Combine. During periods of victory by McMurphy, Bromden's perceptions become clearer, and he recognizes the therapeutic effect of laughter and sheer animal vitality.

The most obvious indication of Bromden's reaction to McMurphy's successes is the temporary shutting down of the fog machine, a nonexistent device, palpably real to Bromden, which grows out of his experience with real fog machines at an English airfield in World War II. Kesey uses it as a recurrent metaphor which serves to elucidate Bromden's ambivalent attitude toward his own madness. The fog machine provides Bromden an excuse to remain camouflaged in a docile role which, because it presents no threat to the Combine, allows him some measure of security. McMurphy's function, which Bromden resists at first, is to draw the Chief out of that refuge into open resistance to the Combine.

When McMurphy does falter momentarily, the possibility that he is little different from the other inmates is seized upon by Bromden with ostensible relief. The word he uses most often to describe McMurphy's behavior during such quiescent periods is "cagey." Bromden sees "caginess" as a necessary and perhaps even admirable trait, the capacity to survive through cunning. He is correct to a limited extent, and it will be his Indian "caginess" which, combined with the physical courage transmitted to him by McMurphy, will enable him to survive. But the word as applied by Bromden in the earlier stages of the book to the total abandonment of struggle against Big Nurse's rule is no more than a euphemism for cowardice. Bromden affects relief at McMurphy's first setbacks and resultant caution because any success on McMurphy's part exposes Bromden to the painful awareness that struggle against the Combine is possible and to the heavy responsibility of trying to be a man. More introspective than ever, Bromden has, under McMurphy's influence, begun a painfully honest reappraisal of his own identity problem:

. . . I'd take a look at my own self in the mirror and wonder

how it was possible that anybody could manage such an enormous thing as being what he was. . . . It don't seem like I
ever have been me. How can McMurphy be what he is?

By accepting society's evaluation of him, Bromden has abdicated the frightening responsibility of
defining himself.[2] Forced by McMurphy's example
to face this responsibility, he is understandably ready
to grasp at any rationalization which will once again
free him from it. Seeing McMurphy acting cagey provides such a rationalization. But no matter how much
Bromden insists upon his admiration for caginess, he
betrays his disappointment subconsciously by an immediate retrogression from his progress toward re-
habilitation each time McMurphy seems beaten or
stalemated. His memories of the tribe become unpleasant, and he remembers how his father, under pressure
from society and his wife, slipped from bold resistance
to caginess to alcoholic defeat: "My Papa was full
Chief. . . . He was real big when I was a kid. My
mother got twice his size. . . . He fought [the Com-
bine] a long time till my mother made him too little to
fight any more and he gave up."

The metaphor of physical size is one which grows
naturally out of the erectile imagery introduced in the
first McMurphy-Bromden meeting. In his hallucinatory understanding of his father's downfall, Bromden
remembers him shrinking in size; and although he
himself is still a physical giant, he perceives himself as
small and weak. In an irony so painful that it loses all
humor, Bromden stands on the floor of the swimming
pool while McMurphy treads water next to him and
blithely tells the reader that McMurphy "must of been
standing in a hole." Again, Bromden tells McMurphy
later, "You're . . . lot bigger . . . 'n I am." It is Mc-
Murphy's stated task to make Bromden "big" again by
making him aware of his own identity.

The swimming pool episode has more far-reaching ramifications. In conversation with the life-guard, McMurphy learns for the first time that he, unlike most of the other inmates, is committed and that his release from the hospital can be withheld in-definitely. A major faltering point for McMurphy follows, with the result that Cheswick, an inmate who had begun to develop resistance to the Combine in emulation of McMurphy, loses all hope and commits suicide by drowning on the next swimming day. This marks the second in a group of three progressively more significant suicides. The first was the self-executed castration of Rawler; the third will be that of Billy Bibbit.

McMurphy's reaction to Cheswick's death and to the concomitant loss of hope by the other patients is not long in coming. After a period of unprecedented personal anguish, he makes the clear moral choice to abandon self-interest and fight the Combine once again. For a time, McMurphy is again in the ascen-dant. The patients begin to gain confidence, and Big Nurse returns to her frighteningly patient biding of time. It is during this period that McMurphy conceives of the fishing trip.

The patients' fishing trip is a hilarious sequence that is significant in the further development of the central characters. Its humor intensifies the tragedy to follow, and the primary symbol which informs it, that of McMurphy as Christ figure, lends substance to the progressive series of moral steps still to be taken by McMurphy. The parallel is drawn most explicitly and with a wry awareness of its overt quality in a conversa-tion between Harding and McMurphy, during which the former explains the procedure of electro shock therapy: "A device that might be said to do the work of the sleeping pill, the electric chair, *and* the torture rack. . . . You are strapped to a table, shaped, ironi-cally, like a cross, with a crown of electric sparks in place of thorns." Toward the book's conclusion, when

McMurphy has brought EST upon himself, he echoes the comparison:

Climbs on the table without any help and spreads his arms out. . . . A switch snaps the clasps on his wrists, ankles, clamping him. . . . They put graphite salve on his temples. "What is it?" he says. "Conductant," the technician says. "Anointest my head with conductant. Do I get a crown of thorns? . . ." Put on those things like headphones, crown of silver thorns. . . .

These are by no means isolated instances of the Christ metaphor. Before the fishing trip, which is attended by twelve followers of McMurphy, including Candy, who is decidedly Magdalene-like in her sweet, generous compassion, Billy Bibbit is advised by his fellow inmate Ellis to "be a fisher of men."

The more significant aspects of McMurphy's role as savior lie not in such simple symbolic leads but in the moral circumstances of his situation. He is, to begin with, fated. Bromden has shown us that no man can meet the Combine head on and escape retribution. Yet McMurphy, a cunning man who prides himself on playing the percentages and on gambling boldly only for personal gain, chooses again and again to fight Big Nurse in increasingly overt ways until his doom is sealed and his victory assured. Kesey takes pains to show us that McMurphy becomes fully aware at an early stage of the conflict that he is dooming himself, an awareness which is echoed (in a humorously melo-dramatic flamboyance) by one of the tattoos on McMurphy's arm: aces and eights, the "dead man's hand."[3] Finally, given an easy opportunity to escape from the hospital near the end of the novel, he refuses by making a transparent excuse of fatigue and allow-ing himself to be trapped by oversleeping. Even when offered a chance to escape further shock treatments and lobotomy by admitting that his actions (and hence his teachings and morality) are wrong, McMurphy refuses.

The significance of McMurphy's hands looms still larger when it begins to coincide with the Christ imagery. McMurphy's hands, already scarred by experience, are cut repeatedly in the course of his hospital stay. One such instance is that of the glass shield. Another, the attempt to lift the control panel, is particularly worthy of note because it is a pivotal episode in the development of the men's loyalty to McMurphy.

At a point when the men are still unwilling to take the risk of voting with McMurphy for the privilege of watching the World Series on television, he maneuvers them into a discussion of possible escape methods and then into a bet on whether he is capable of lifting a massive, obsolete control panel, formerly used to regulate water therapy and resembling a torture device. It is four hundred pounds of steel and concrete, no longer of any use to the Combine; but during McMurphy's attempt to lift it (and finally in Bromden's successful use of it as a battering ram in his escape), it comes to represent the monolithic weight of the Combine, a machinery which claims to be invulnerable to the efforts of any single man to move it.

The men, all of whom have lost money to McMurphy gambling, seize gleefully on the sure bet he offers them. As at the end of the book, McMurphy fails physically but wins a clear moral victory.

His whole body shakes with the strain as he tries to lift something he *knows* he can't lift, something *everybody* knows he can't lift. . . . Then his breath explodes out of him, and he falls back limp. . . . There's blood on the levers where he tore his hands . . . he fishes in his pockets for all the IOU's he won the last few days at poker. . . . "But I tried, though," he says.

The attempt provides an insight into McMurphy's character for the inmates as well as the reader. The lesson that one must strive to be and do more than one thinks he can is one of the more important aspects of the legacy McMurphy will leave them. Furthermore, he has given the lie to his often-proclaimed policy of shrewd self-interest and at the same time given the others a taste of victory by letting them win back their money. The immediate result is that those present do vote for the World Series proposal, including Bromden, for whom it is a daring step back into the world.

Bromden has said only a giant could lift the control panel. Later he sees McMurphy as a "giant come out of the sky to save us." By the conclusion of the novel, Bromden has come to realize that this is a false evaluation and a false hope. Despite his size and strength, his courage and colossal vitality, the flamboyant mannerisms which make him resemble a comic-book hero, McMurphy is not a giant but a man; and Bromden's salvation will come from within.

Bromden has idealized McMurphy, but Nurse Ratched makes an equally great error in underestimating him. In a meeting with the medical staff (whom she dominates), she defines McMurphy pejoratively in terms of his humanity: "I don't agree that he is some kind of extraordinary being—some kind of 'super' psychopath. . . . He is simply a man and no more, and is subject to all the fears and all the cowardice and all the timidity that any other man is subject to." McMurphy is most certainly subject to human fears and weaknesses. The difference between him and the "rabbits" who have hitherto constituted Big Nurse's experience with inmates is that he refuses to be governed and debilitated by these limitations. Despite McMurphy's recognition of his own vulnerability and mortality, he sets himself to a constant testing of the limits of the human condition. Although he is not superhuman, he does show himself to be extraordinary.

Big Nurse has smugly dismissed McMurphy as "simply a man and no more," but by the climax of their confrontation he will have shown her that being a man, rising to the heights of human potential, is enough. In addition, he will demonstrate that she is no invincible machine but simply a woman, a human being with all the attendant human vulnerability and fallibility.

At one point, during McMurphy's temporary absence from the ward, Big Nurse asks the patients whether they consider him "a martyr or a saint." They agree that he is neither, and in pressing her point (the essential self-interest which she feels is McMurphy's constant motivation), she reiterates these terms several times. The consummate irony, of course, is that McMurphy, for all his pretensions to the role of cunning con man, is to rise to heights of selfless sacrifice bordering on the saintly, while Big Nurse, smugly confident of her own moral superiority, reaches the nadir of her function as agent of repression. By underestimating the commitment and courage of which her adversary is capable, she undertakes a struggle which is to end in a true martyrdom for him and in her own irrevocable defeat.

Other references to Christ and Christianity which seem at first to bear no consistent relationship to the pattern which attaches to McMurphy emerge finally as part of a sophisticated statement on organized religion. One of these is provided by the inmate Ellis who, his sensibilities bludgeoned by repeated EST treatments, stands perpetually in the attitude of crucifixion. One of the Combine's most bizarre failures, Ellis is a clearly symbolic example of the atrocities it commits in the name of society.

Still more revealing of Kesey's intent is the treatment of another peripheral character, the anxiety-ridden Nurse Pilbow. A devout Catholic, she has a morbid fear of sex and a hatred of her patients, especially McMurphy, whom she considers a sex maniac. The tangible representation of Miss Pilbow's repressed sexuality is her hideous purple birthmark, which is itself the subject of one of Bromden's hallucinatory perceptions of truth. Pilbow persists in the attempt to externalize evil. Her denial of her sexual instincts has resulted in hatred and fear rather than love and acceptance. Her rigidly proscriptive morality, when held in ludicrous juxtaposition to McMurphy's guiltless, relaxed, and fertile pleasure in life, suggests that the organized church has failed to bring the essential Christian message of love to the people. And in perpetrating the kind of rigid morality which has scarred not only Pilbow but most of the inmates, organized religion has become an arm of the Combine.

McMurphy, in opposing this, is performing a function similar to that of Christ: attacking an outmoded morality and sweeping away its hypocrisies while assimilating and perpetuating its positive aspects in a new moral code. Thus, although McMurphy espouses an apparently amoral sexuality, he infuses his followers with a brotherly love which is distinctly Christian and which a mechanistic society has forgotten.

From the outset, McMurphy has been aware that guerrilla action is the method by which Big Nurse may be harassed safely. But as Miss Ratched, after losing a few hands, calmly continues to raise the stakes from behind her mechanical poker face, McMurphy is forced to choose between backing off and calling her bluff.

What keeps the contest from becoming either morbidly dull or unbearably terrifying to the reader is Kesey's capacity to render absurd humor. Toward the end of the book, Harding says of the farewell party for McMurphy, "It isn't happening. It's all a collaboration of Kafka and Mark Twain. . . ." and one gets the idea that Kesey extends this judgment to the entire world of the Combine.

It is in this spirit of easygoing humor that McMurphy begins to break through Bromden's defenses and draw him back into the world. Although the central improvement in Bromden is psychological, its outward manifestations are tied to the metaphor of physical size and potency. When the partially reclaimed Bromden lies awake, anxious to go on the fishing trip, McMurphy talks to him and offers to make him "big" again. After listening to McMurphy describe the two whores who are coming on the trip, Bromden experiences his first erection in many years; and McMurphy, pulling back the blankets, bawdily puns, "look there, Chief. . . . You growed a half a foot already." The pun is significantly close to literal truth, for sexual potency is shown as both a symptom and a function of masculine identity; Bromden's new self-awareness will result in a fearsome potency which thwarts the Combine and its agents, combined with a commitment to his fellow inmates which spells hope for all men.

After the fishing trip, events proceed rapidly and inexorably to a conclusion. Although the trip is a great success for the men, who return to an awareness of a more primitive, active, fertile world and bring that awareness back to contaminate and erode the sterility of the hospital, McMurphy pays a high personal price. Pushing and carrying them back to life drains his stores of vitality. During the drive back to the hospital, he entertains the men with tales of his exploits: "[he] doled out his life for us to live . . . full of . . . loving women and barroom battles over meager honors. . . ." But the lights of a passing car reveal to Bromden that McMurphy's face looks "dreadfully tired and strained and *frantic*, like there wasn't enough time left for something he had to do. . . ." McMurphy is clearly aware that the men are feeding vicariously off his energies and is even more acutely aware of the greater sacrifice to come. But, as Bromden later points out, McMurphy could never have avoided the final battle because, as is shown by his memory of "barroom battles over *meager* honors," he knows that in life the fight itself is what matters.

The battle lines are drawn by the agents of the Combine; but instead of demoralizing the men, this pulls them closer together. In defense of another inmate, and with resignation rather than anger, McMurphy allows an orderly to goad him into a fistfight which he knows will provide Big Nurse the excuse she needs to bring more formidable weapons into play. Perhaps more significant is the fact that Bromden, accepting responsibility for his fellow man, steps in to help McMurphy when he is outnumbered.

From this point on, Bromden is his own man, growing in strength as McMurphy declines. The two go together to the EST room. For Bromden, this shock treatment, his last ever, is a turning point. With McMurphy as an example, he fights his panic, takes his treatment, and then works his way back out of the fog, never to hide in it again. Bromden returns to the ward to be greeted as a hero by the other men, largely assuming McMurphy's former position, while McMurphy, the focus of Big Nurse's vengeance, undergoes repeated shock treatments.

With no end to the treatments in sight and Big Nurse considering more drastic methods, it is decided that McMurphy's escape from the hospital must be engineered. McMurphy agrees but insists on postponing his departure until after a secret midnight visit from Candy and her friend Sandy, which turns into a farewell party, fueled by cocktails made of codeine-based cough syrup and a few friendly tokes of marijuana with Mr. Turkle.

The party is a success on every level. Billy Bibbit loses his virginity to Candy in the seclusion room, the men draw closer together and begin to entertain hopes of overcoming the control of the Combine, and McMurphy's escape before dawn, using Turkle's key to unlock a window, is assured. Bromden articulates the full significance of the rebellion: "I had to keep reminding myself that it had *truly* happened, that we had made it happen. . . . Maybe the Combine wasn't all-powerful." But although they have in the past overestimated the strength of the Combine and Big Nurse, this time Bromden and the others have underestimated it. It is only McMurphy who still recognizes the extent of the control held over the men and understands the fact that his own complete sacrifice is necessary to effect their freedom. He decides to take a nap before leaving, "accidentally" oversleeps, and is discovered by the morning staff.

In retrospect, Bromden is able to understand McMurphy's motives and the inevitability of the events to follow:

. . . it was bound to be and would have happened in one way or another . . . even if Mr. Turkle had got McMurphy . . . off the ward like was planned. . . . McMurphy would have . . . come back . . . he could [not] have . . . let the Big Nurse have the last move. . . . It was like he'd signed on for the whole game. . . .

When Billy Bibbit is discovered asleep in Candy's arms (a scene notable for its childlike innocence), Big Nurse proceeds to barrage him with recriminations until the old habit patterns of guilt and dependence are reawakened. Moments later, Billy commits suicide by cutting his throat.

Nurse Ratched's reaction is typical of her smug confidence in the infallibility of her own Combine-sanctioned values. She lays the blame immediately at McMurphy's feet. Bromden watches him

. . . in his chair in the corner, resting a second before he came out for the next round. . . . The thing he was fighting, you couldn't whip it for good. All you could do was keep on whipping it, till you couldn't come out any more and some-body else had to take your place.

Bromden is the man who will take McMurphy's place, and because of this he understands what Mc-Murphy must do. He is acting as an agent for all the

men, and as Bromden realizes, "We couldn't stop him
because we were the ones making him do it." In his
final, physical attack on Nurse Ratched, McMurphy
rips her starched uniform off, tearing down her insula-
tion as he did with the glass wall, exposing her large,
fleshy breasts, and making it clear that she is a
vulnerable woman rather than an invincible machine.
She will never again command absolute power over
the inmates.

The aftermath is the complete disintegration of
Miss Ratched's rule. Most of the men sign themselves
out, but Bromden postpones his departure because he
suspects that Big Nurse may make one last play. He is
correct: One day, McMurphy, now a vegetable after
undergoing a lobotomy (perhaps the ultimate castration), is wheeled back into the ward. In a scene
characterized by an intense intimacy, Bromden per-
forms a merciful service for McMurphy, smothering
him to death. The transfer of power is complete.
Bromden picks up McMurphy's hat, tries it on, and
finds it too small. He feels "ashamed" at trying to wear
it because he knows that McMurphy has taught him
that one must find one's own identity. Then he picks
up the control panel, smashes it through a window,
and makes his escape.

Bromden is McMurphy's most successful disciple.
It is not until the very end of the novel, however, that
it becomes clear that Bromden has surpassed his
teacher in the capacity to survive in American society
and to maintain personal identity in spite of the Combine. It must be remembered that Bromden is a half-
breed and that this mixed heritage has been a major
contributing factor to his severe alienation and identity problems. But Bromden shows that his half-breed
status also represents a capacity to combine the
strengths of both the Indian and the white man. From
his father he inherited a functional cunning, a patient
caution which in its original form was conducive to

both survival and pride. Although this quality has been perverted into the fearful "caginess" he once practiced and professed to admire, it is, in a less extreme form, a valuable attribute.

From the first page, it is clear that Bromden has long practiced the tactic of evasion against the onslaughts of the Combine. The price he has paid in loss of pride and identity obscures for a time the undeniable fact that he is the only man who has *fooled* the Combine successfully: Big Nurse and her staff believe that Bromden is a deaf-mute, and he is able to eavesdrop safely on their most private dealings. McMurphy, because he fights the Combine head-on, dies; but Bromden, who learns to practice a fusion of evasive cunning and sheer courage, survives as the hope for the future.

It is clear that one need not have the physical prowess of a McMurphy or a Bromden to renounce rabbithood and become a man. Kesey suggests that someone like Dale Harding has a very real chance to thwart the Combine, and even Billy Bibbit is able to go part of the way. Despite Billy's failure, Kesey's feeling is clear: It is better to be destroyed in the attempt to fight the Combine than to accept the role of rabbit for life.

Randle Patrick McMurphy is a compelling figure. Into the sterility of Bromden's world and the stifling American society it represents, he brings a breath, a breeze, a wind of change. In the wasteland of the ward, his sexual vitality makes him loom as a figure of mythic proportions. Yet the most important part of the legacy he has left Bromden and his fellows is that he was just a man. And that, finally, is enough.

3

Two Followed after the Cuckoo's Nest: Stage and Screen Adaptations

On November 13, 1963, a stage adaptation of *One Flew Over the Cuckoo's Nest* written by Dale Wasserman opened at the Cort Theatre in New York. The production starred Kirk Douglas as McMurphy, with Joan Tetzel as Nurse Ratched and Gene Wilder as Billy Bibbit. The play received unfavorable reviews and closed after three months. In 1969, a revised version opened in San Francisco and enjoyed far greater success, as did the 1971 off-Broadway production at the Mercer-Hansberry Theatre, starring William Devane and Janet Ward. Since then, Wasserman's play has been performed by various amateur and professional companies around the country to great popular success.

Kirk Douglas had bought the movie rights to *Cuckoo's Nest* from Kesey in 1962 for $18,000. For years, rumors circulated that the making of the film was imminent. Finally, Douglas turned the rights over to his son, Michael. Michael Douglas and Saul Zaentz produced the movie in 1975. At the 1976 Academy Awards it won five Oscars: best picture, best director (Milos Forman), best actor (Jack Nicholson as McMurphy), best actress (Louise Fletcher as Nurse Ratched), and best screenplay adapted from another medium (Lawrence Hauben and Bo Goldman).

This last award carries some irony for Kesey and his admirers. Kesey himself had been hired to write the screenplay, but after the initial drafts he and the producers parted company under less than amicable circumstances. Kesey's subsequent successful lawsuit was based on the premise that he had not consented to the use of his name in connection with the final version of the film[1]; but the primary artistic disagreement seems to have been over the producers' decision to shoot the film from a realistic, almost documentary point of view, even to the extent of casting some real patients in minor roles and Dean Brooks, director of Oregon State Hospital in Salem, where the movie was shot, as Dr. Spivey. Kesey had wanted to retain the hallucinatory point of view of Chief Bromden.[2]

I believe that this shift in point of view is the essential weakness in a movie that has many strengths. As Jack Kroll wrote in *Newsweek*:

The result is a well-made film that flares at times into incandescence but lacks ultimately the novel's passion, insight and complexity. . . . Kesey's novel was filtered through the paranoid consciousness of his Indian narrator, Chief Bromden. By opting for a style of comic realism, Forman loses much of the nightmare quality that made the book a capsized allegory of an increasingly mad reality.[3]

I have dealt at some length with the significance of Bromden's point of view. This significance was recognized by Dale Wasserman when he wrote the stage version. At frequent intervals, Chief Bromden stands alone on a dark stage as a single shaft of light falls on him and "vague and milky light-patterns wreathe and intertwine across the stage" while his inner thoughts (represented by his voice on a tape) address his dead father:

Papa? They're foggin' it in again. . . . You hear it, Papa? The Black Machine. . . . They're puttin' people in one end and out comes what they want. . . . You think I'm ravin' 'cause it sounds too awful to be true, but, my *God*, there's such a lot of things that's true even if they never really happen![4]

This emphasis on Bromden and his madness, including a reference to the fog machine and a paraphrase of Bromden's words from the novel, is symptomatic of the greater fidelity of the play to the novel. The movie departs more radically and frequently from the novel, but director Forman has thus succeeded to a greater degree in presenting a work of some originality and artistic merit in its own right.

Both Forman (with screenwriters Goldman and Hauben) and Wasserman have made various alterations, compressions, and omissions of necessity in adapting *Cuckoo's Nest* to the limitations and strengths of their chosen media. Some characters are omitted in each version (e.g., George Sorensen appears in neither) and others are combined (as in Wasserman's effective merging of Ruckley with Ellis). Some clearly recognizable characters have undergone inexplicable changes of name. Thus, in the play, Nurse Pilbow becomes Nurse Flinn, and Aide Washington becomes Williams. In the movie, Pilbow and Washington retain their original names, but Aide Geever becomes Miller, and Sandy becomes Rose. More puzzling is the large role written into the movie for Taber, a character who did not live on the ward during McMurphy's stay but is remembered by Bromden as an unsuccessful precursor to McMurphy, a less forceful rebel who was ultimately defeated by the Combine. The Combine is not even mentioned in the movie, and Taber is a loud, exuberant psychotic whose barely contained violence clearly is less controllable than McMurphy's. Perhaps he represents that true madness which McMurphy never evinces; ironically, he survives McMurphy's destruction to give the exultant shout of triumph at the film's conclusion when Bromden escapes.

Along with their limitations, both stage and screen media enjoy some advantages over fiction. The visual immediacy of Bromden smothering McMurphy in both versions, the graphic representation of McMurphy's EST convulsions, particularly in the movie close-up, and the appearance of the patients are very effective. The play's success with audiences lies in the essential dramatic power of the plot situation itself, which sweeps one along in its own forceful movement, despite such omissions as the fishing trip.

Excellent casting is one of the movie's great strengths. In addition to the verisimilitude lent by the use of real patients and psychiatrist in a real hospital, casting directors Mike Fenton and Jane Feinberg filled most roles almost perfectly. Among the patients, Brad Dourif is superb as Billy Bibbit. Almost as good are Sydney Lassick as Cheswick (although the character does not commit suicide in either adaptation) and William Redfield as Harding. Will Sampson is everyone's idea of Chief Bromden, and Scatman Crothers is a fine Turkle, disarmingly humorous in his vices.

Jack Nicholson and Louise Fletcher give excellent performances as McMurphy and Ratched, effectively overcoming the preconceptions of faithful readers of the novel, despite the fact that neither is a physically accurate representation of Kesey's character. For one thing, neither is big enough. Nicholson is not the broad, muscular McMurphy who inspires Bromden to think a giant has come to save him. Fletcher is too slender and attractive to suggest the invincible machine that Ratched is to Bromden. Thus, we are not tempted even briefly to see these characters as mythic figures, larger than life, the revelation of whose human vulnerability is so important to the novel's conclusion. Nonetheless, Nicholson's enormous, infectious vitality makes his McMurphy a forceful, engaging creation. And Fletcher, her pompadour resembling horns, uses subtle facial expressions—smug self-righteousness, rigidly controlled rage, a smirk half hidden by a hand—to evoke a Ratched whom anyone can hate.

In their ages, too, the characters differ from their counterparts in the novel. Ratched is no longer fifteen years older than McMurphy. Rather, Forman seems intentionally to have made them contemporaries. This, coupled with Fletcher's undeniably attractive appearance, heightens the sexual tensions between the antagonists, particularly the graphically sexual suggestion of the climactic strangulation scene, when Nicholson lies on top of the struggling Fletcher.

Finally, it should be noted that in casting Louise Fletcher for the role, Forman has robbed the character of a primary ambiguity of motive that enriched the novel. Kesey's Big Nurse appears an invincible monster to Bromden. The climactic scene in which McMurphy reveals her humanity holds great import for Bromden and the reader, and it opens the further question of whether the nurse is a consciously evil character or a self-deluding bureaucrat who believes that she is doing good. In showing Fletcher as a rigid, tight-lipped, but clearly human woman—with a first name, Mildred— Forman imposes his own resolution of this interesting ambiguity, showing her as a misguided person who believes in her own good intentions. Jack Kroll points out that "Most of the characters are thinned out. . . . Big Nurse, deprived of most of her mythic dimension, seems much more of a sexist concept—Woman as Castrator."[5] Thus, paradoxically, the humanization of Ratched does not add a more humanistic dimension to the film.

I have said that Wasserman's play is more faithful to the novel. Not only is Bromden's hallucinatory perspective maintained, including his references to the fog machine and the Combine, but the wild geese pass overhead in the scene during which he begins to find himself. In the movie, Bromden's character is simplified: He is not insane but merely a cunning Indian who has fooled the medical staff for years by pretending to be deaf and dumb. His first speech, upon accepting a stick of Juicy Fruit gum from McMurphy, is played largely for laughs; and the development of his relationship with McMurphy seems less credible, sudden rather than gradual.

The play also retains references to lobotomy as castration, to Nurse Ratched as a destructive mother, and to the Christ imagery of the EST scene. Many passages are taken almost verbatim from the novel, including the children's rhyme of the title, which is spoken as Bromden undergoes EST. Some speeches are retained but shifted to a different point in the action. Because of this, in at least one case a line is quoted entirely out of context, thus garbling Kesey's intention: McMurphy tells Bromden, "You growed half a foot already,"[6] but the preceding passage about young women has been shifted to a later point so that the bawdy but significant double entendre is lost.

In departing dramatically from the novel, Milos Forman has taken some chances. Often he succeeds in doing something as well as or better than Kesey. The fishing trip (of necessity omitted from the play) enables Forman to use the advantages peculiar to his medium. The contrast between the constriction of the locked ward—in which almost all camera shots are tightly framed close-ups—and the enormous expanse of an incredibly blue sea in an extreme long shot state far better than words the polarity between the repression of Nurse Ratched's ward and the freedom McMurphy offers the men. These two settings suggest too the dual strengths of Forman's work. He is able to present both a dispassionate, depressing docu-drama and an exultant fictive story.

Similarly, Forman moves the basketball game outside, from the ward in which Kesey set it to an exercise yard which, while fenced in, is open to the sky. The surrounding trees and the image of a squirrel running atop the fence suggest that this is an interim stage between imprisonment and freedom. Indeed, McMurphy later escapes from the yard to steal a bus and take his fellow inmates fishing. And it is in the exercise yard, in two different basketball scenes, that Bromden's movement toward confidence and freedom under McMurphy's tutelage is implied. In the first scene, McMurphy is able only to get Bromden to raise his hands with the basketball, not to dunk it, though he demonstrates by climbing onto Bancini's shoulders. Here, McMurphy literally shows Bromden how to be big, as he looks down on him. The scene is effectively bracketed by two shots of Nurse Ratched looking silently down on both of them, framed ghostlike and forbidding by the ward window. In the second basketball scene, the actual game with the aides, Bromden gradually blossoms until he becomes the star of the game, obviously delighted with himself.

The first basketball scene suggests a juxtaposition of two symbols from the novel: hands and windows. In the novel, the two are linked when McMurphy shatters the window of the nurses' station with his hand, and the recurrent symbolism of the hand radiates outward from that center. Forman does less with hands, but he creates a pervasive and effective pattern of windows and television sets. Upon McMurphy's first appearance on the ward, Forman uses a wide-angle lens for a tightly framed shot of his handcuffed hands from below. They seem red and very large, and the implicit phallic symbolism is emphasized when McMurphy hooks one finger in his fly. Later, as McMurphy leans against the window of the nurses' station, Ratched tells him, "Your hand is staining my window." In addition to raising his hands with the basketball, Chief Bromden raises one hand to vote for the World Series after McMurphy suggestively exhorts him, "All the guys have got 'em up. . . . Show her that you can still do it, Chief."

McMurphy's shattering of Nurse Ratched's window is less effective in the movie than in the novel.

Kesey presented it as a conscious act, dispassionately chosen by McMurphy to mark a new stage in the escalation of his rebellion. Forman loses much of its significance, presenting it as a sudden, impulsive act of frustration, wedged into a series of telescoped events which move the plot along rapidly, achieving compression at the expense of emphasis. Within a few minutes, McMurphy learns he is committed indefinitely, momentarily considers acting cagey, is faced with Nurse Ratched's withholding of cigarettes and Cheswick's tantrum about that issue, and breaks the window. This precipitates his fight with Washington, Warren's interference, Bromden's aiding of McMurphy, their assignment to the EST room, the first conversation between McMurphy and Bromden, and their decision to escape to Canada together.

Forman is more subtle in his recurrent use of windows. In addition to the scenes already mentioned, windows figure in a pattern of escapes and attempted escapes. Candy and Rose enter through a window, promising both figurative and literal escape through the same window. Ultimately, Bromden does escape by shattering the window. Finally, television sets are seen as pseudo-windows. When Nurse Ratched refuses to allow McMurphy to watch the World Series, he is shown looking disconsolately at his reflection in the dead TV screen. Remembering who he is, he perks up and begins cheering. Soon he is joined by Martini, and both their faces are reflected. When the others join them, they all momentarily escape Big Nurse's rule through the television set. Later, on the fishing trip, the men look fearfully and hungrily out of the bus windows at the outside world. Each is framed in his own window, isolated. They pass an appliance store outside which, in a palpably ironic shot, several older people are comfortably seated, looking through the store window at a daytime television show. Despite their ostensible freedom, these people have chosen to watch flickering shadows rather than participate in life. But the patients themselves soon choose life in the fishing episode which follows.

It is in this choice of life, freedom, and vitality, clearly implicit in the beautifully photographed fishing sequence, that Forman most effectively captures the exuberant hope of Kesey's vision. And the film's conclusion, when Bromden laboriously rips the hydrotherapy machine from its moorings, lifts it with palpably gathering confidence, crashes it through the window, and gradually disappears into the breaking dawn, his white pajama legs moving ethereally like wings, is easily as moving as the same conclusion in Kesey's words. It is far more effective than Wasserman's conclusion, in which, after shorting out the hospital's power by lifting the control panel, Bromden leaves through a window that Harding unlocks for him.

Although neither adaptation can consistently approach the level of artistic success achieved in the novel, both have virtues and lapses. Ultimately, however, Wasserman's play, with all its gestures toward fidelity to the original, is relatively pedestrian and unimaginative in conception, while Forman's movie, its omissions and departures from the novel notwithstanding, is more admirable as an independent and original work of art.

Unfortunately, the same cannot be said of the movie version of *Sometimes a Great Notion*, which merits no more than a brief mention. Released in 1971, the film stars Paul Newman as Hank Stamper, Henry Fonda as Henry, and Lee Remick as Viv, with Michael Sarrazin as Lee and Richard Jaeckel as Joby. In compressing the massive, complex novel into a two-hour movie, director Paul Newman made no apparent attempt to create more than an entertaining cinematic plot summary. Because of this unpretentious approach and its excellent cast, the movie is moderately successful as an entertainment; but it bears only the most superficial resemblance to Kesey's fine work. Further liberties were taken when the movie came to network television. The title was changed to "Never Give a Inch," and so many plot transitions were cut to make room for commercials that the movie became incomprehensible to viewers unfamiliar with the novel or the full-length version. Particularly ill served was the potentially fine role of Viv, which was cut and simplified to the point where even the considerable talents of Lee Remick could not make the character's motivation clear. In short, this movie is no more than a simplistic popularization of Kesey's finest work.

4

Sometimes a Great Notion:
The Force of Will

Despite the greater popularity of *One Flew Over the Cuckoo's Nest*, Kesey's second novel, *Sometimes a Great Notion*, is a far more artistically impressive work on several levels. In terms of structure, point of view, and theme, it is more ambitious, more experimental, and ultimately more successful.

The primary movement of the book is similar to that of *Cuckoo's Nest*, with one significant distinction: Where the emphasis in the first novel is upon the *transfer* of power from McMurphy to Bromden, the fall of one man and the rise of another, *Notion* posits a *fusion* of the strengths of two half-brothers, Lee and Hank Stamper, who force each other to become complete human beings.

The intensity of the relationship between Lee and Hank is to be understood primarily in terms of their bizarre relationships to Lee's mother, Myra, and to their father, Henry. After the death of Hank's unremarkable and unremarked mother, Henry Stamper, the head of a tough family of Oregon lumberjacks, travels to New York, where he woos and weds Myra, a twenty-one-year-old Stanford co-ed home on vacation. At this time, Henry is fifty-one years old, Hank ten. Two years later, Leland (Lee) Stanford Stamper is born to Myra and Henry. On Hank's sixteenth birthday, Myra rebels against the

lonely ruggedness of her life with an aging, taciturn
husband by seducing the youth. Their sexual relationship continues for years, until she takes Lee east to
school. Lee is twelve years old at this time, and his
hatred and fear of Hank are fed by the fact that he has
witnessed, through a hole in his room, the sexual activity of Myra and his older brother. Hank is by now a
grown man, and the situation presents classically
Oedipal problems for Lee.

The major action of the novel takes place twelve
years later, after Myra's suicide, when Lee, now a
twenty-four-year-old graduate student at Yale, leaves
behind a crumbling academic career and an abortive
suicide attempt of his own to return to Oregon (at
Hank's cryptic invitation) to help the shorthanded
family logging business meet a deadline.

During Lee's twelve-year absence, Hank has mar-
ried Viv, unquestionably the most successfully drawn,
most admirable female character in Kesey's work. A
remarkable woman who embodies both ruggedness
and sensitivity, Viv represents a combination of both
brothers' best qualities. Lee's plan for vengeance upon
Hank involves "pulling him down" rather than trying
to "measure up" to him, and the method he chooses is
the seduction of Viv. Although he appears to succeed,
the emotional consequences of Lee's plan are far different from what he intended. For one thing, Viv has a
will of her own. Although she loves both brothers, she
ultimately concludes that they have used her as a sur-
rogate for Myra and decides to leave them both. For
another, the depth of love felt for Viv by both Lee and
Hank intensifies their conflict with each other, and
both ultimately learn to "measure up," to be more
than they had thought necessary or desirable. Hank is
forced to recognize that courage and stoicism must be
tempered by sensitivity and compassion. Lee comes to
see that his aesthetic cynicism has been an affectation
intended to hide his cowardice; he chooses courage
instead.

The emotional environment in which the confrontation between the brothers takes place is conditioned by the intense hostility of all the townspeople of Wakonda, Oregon, toward the Stampers. Hank, in a characteristically stubborn, individualistic decision, has agreed to supply the Wakonda Pacific lumber company with logs, thus frustrating the aims of the striking loggers' union. The sagging economy of Wakonda affects the lives of all its inhabitants, and each resents Hank Stamper personally, from Simone, the prostitute, to Jonathan Bailey Draeger, the union president.

As the disapproval of the community and the difficulty of filling the logging contract grow, Hank's support from the extended Stamper family erodes, until only cousin Joby (who is more like a brother to Hank) and a distant relative named Andy remain on the job. After a catastrophe in the state park in which Joby is killed and old Henry mortally injured, Hank returns home to find Lee in bed with Viv. Weakened by illness, overwork, grief, and a beating administered by union goons, Hank seems ready to accept defeat. But after further provocation from malicious townsfolk and from Lee, Hank renews his defiance. Hank and Lee purge their rage and fear in a fistfight. Grappling in a ritualistic, dancelike embrace, they draw closer together than ever before; and as their blood literally mingles in the struggle, they complete their fusion, a union of East and West, urbane and countrified, cerebral and physical. Each has forced the other to become complete.

As the novel ends, Lee and Hank are embarking on the Herculean task of delivering the logs to Wakonda Pacific, while Viv leaves them both behind in her search for a life and an identity of her own. And a grotesque symbol hangs from a pole at the Stamper house: old Henry's amputated arm, fist up with the middle finger extended, a battle pennant shouting silent defiance to the union, the town, and the world.

In a letter to his friend Ken Babbs, written during the composition of *Cuckoo's Nest*, Kesey stated: "I'll discuss point of view for a time now. I am beginning to agree with Stegner, that it truely [sic] is the most important problem in writing."[1] He went on to discuss his decision to change the point of view of *Cuckoo's Nest* from third person omniscient to something resembling its final, first-person form. In *Sometimes a Great Notion*, Kesey refused to limit himself to either technique. Although the novel is written primarily in the third person, sudden shifts into first-person narrative from the point of view of each major character occur throughout. In addition, Kesey employs conscious authorial intrusion by introducing his chapters with italicized passages, conversational in tone, addressed directly from the author to the reader:[2]

STOP! DON'T SWEAT IT. SIMPLY MOVE A FEW INCHES LEFT OR RIGHT TO GET A NEW VIEWPOINT. . . . Truth doesn't run on time like a commuter train, though time may run on truth. And the Scenes Gone By and the Scenes to Come flow blending together in the seagreen deep while Now spreads in circles on the surface. So don't sweat it. For focus simply move a few inches back or forward. And once more . . . look:

As the barroom explodes gently outward into the rain, in spreading spherical waves:

Dusty Kansas train depot in 1898.

This passage, clearly suggestive of cinematic devices, is interesting not only in terms of point of view but also for the insight it gives us to Kesey's structural technique in *Notion*. In a complex but dramatically effective plot structure, Kesey weaves several temporal planes in and out of one another, shifting them in as deceptively careless a manner as he does point of view. The narrative begins and ends on Thanksgiving Day 1961, the climactic day when Viv leaves Oregon and Hank and Lee begin the attempt to transport their cut logs down the Wakonda Auga river. In between, the

focus moves constantly back and forth between the
beginning of the Stamper family history and the present. This in itself is not unusual, but the almost cinematic rapidity, smoothness, and clarity with which
Kesey presents these shifts are. Above all, Kesey's control is impressive as he gradually conveys to the reader
a sense of omniscience, a feeling that we are privy to
the entire Stamper saga, unhampered by temporal or
geographic limitations:

The old boltcutter props the rim of his glass of port against
his lower lip and tips in the wine, watching grayly from the
dusty gloom. The postman crosses a bright green lawn in New
Haven, holding the card. The old house, shimmering and
tiny under the dawn sky, like a pebble beneath an abalone
shell, opens to emit two figures in logging garb.

As Tony Tanner points out in *City of Words*,
Kesey intends to give the "illusion of temporal and
spacial simultaneity."[3] This narrative device is most
concentrated in the development of Lee, who remarks
early in the novel: ". . . looking back I remember the
depot, the gas, the bus trip, the blast . . . all these
scenes as one scene, composed of dozens of simultaneously occurring events. . . ." He continues, in
retrospect: "I could now . . . arrange them in accurate chronological order . . . but being accurate is
not necessarily being honest."

Lee recognizes, as does the reader, the greater
depth afforded his experience by this simultaneity. But
there are points at which it is distressing to him.
Awakened before dawn in his childhood bedroom
after his first night back in Oregon, Lee is confused:

. . . I was able to establish the *where* but not the
when. . . . And the raw materials of reality without that
glue of time are materials adrift and reality is as meaningless
as the balsa parts of a model airplane scattered to the
wind. . . . What year is it? . . . it took at least the first two
weeks of my stay to gather all the balsawood pieces—longer
than that to glue them into any order again.

In returning to the scene of his childhood trauma, Lee hopes to purge it. In order to do so, he is forced (as was Bromden) to remember, even relive, childhood experiences. The painful fragmentation he undergoes in doing so is a necessary prelude to the ultimate integration of self which he seeks. An example of this process occurs midway through the book, on Halloween, a day which, like Thanksgiving, represents one of the primary temporal focal points of the novel. Trapped on the beach by several teenage hoodlums who force him into the cold water, Lee is rescued by Hank. During the episode, he experiences a flashback to a Halloween of his childhood, when Hank rescued him from a "devil's stovepipe," a deep pit into which he had fallen. The juxtaposition of the two parallel situations forces Lee to recognize aspects of his ambivalent relationship to his brother and to move closer to self-knowledge. Although the teenagers run from Hank "as if the devil were after them," Hank functions as a savior to Lee. In the devil's stovepipe scene, Hank has saved Lee from a plunge into hell. On the beach in 1961, he enables him to emerge from the ocean as though baptized, ready to learn a new conception of self. The experience represents a crucial turning point for Lee. Although he will retrogress at times, he begins at this point to move toward an honest self-appraisal.

If the gathering maturity of Kesey's structural technique in *Notion* is impressive and gratifying to the reader, the greater sophistication of his character development and thematic statements must be equally so. Although Kesey again is concerned with the expression of individual identity in the face of repressive forces, the portrayal of that individuality is rendered in terms of wider human possibilities than in *Cuckoo's Nest*. To be sure, Hank Stamper, a man similar in many respects to McMurphy, is again the clearest representative of individualism. But Hank learns more and changes more profoundly from Lee's influence than McMurphy did from that of Bromden or Harding. Not merely sensitivity and cerebration but humility and even the admission of weakness are necessary, as Hank ultimately realizes, to the development of a man. Yet the awareness of one's vulnerability does not obviate the moral responsibility to make meaningful choices in one's life and, by acting upon them, to define oneself existentially. These realizations are a long time in coming to Hank, given the rigidity of the Stamper ethic transmitted to him by his father.

Hank's paternal grandfather, Jonas, was an atypical Stamper. Self-righteously religious, lacking the stoicism characteristic of the family and of Henry in particular, he was defeated by the hostile environment of Oregon and deserted his family to return to Kansas. His pious pronouncements and the disgrace which Henry feels his weakness cast upon the family make him, even in absence, a major negative example for Stamper behavior in Henry's teachings to Hank. The clash of two opposed ideologies is conveyed strikingly in Henry's response to Jonas's gift, mailed from Kansas, to his newborn grandson. It is a wall plaque, a "copper bas-relief of Jesus . . . and raised copper letters declaring, 'Blessed Are the Meek. . . .' " Henry, with fierce humor, immediately paints the plaque with yellow machine paint and crudely letters "his own personal gospel over the raised copper words of Jesus," then nails the plaque to the wall of Hank's room, where it remains throughout his formative years, proclaiming Henry's philosophy, which becomes Hank's as well: "NEVER GIVE A INCH!"

Hank lives by this Stamper dictum; but the plaque's original message is not entirely lost. At night, there is a braille effect, as Hank explains: ". . . them curlicue words you could read with your fingers at night when the lights went out, 'Blessed are the meek' and so forth and so on." On Hank's sixteenth birthday, before the consummation of their relationship, Myra

explains to Hank the pervasive effect the plaque has
had upon his life. The lingering braille message and
the influence of Myra prefigure the advent not of Viv,
who will not succeed in changing Hank's vision dras-
tically, but of Lee, who will.

Hank's refusal to give an inch, ever, applies to the
world at large, to all forces, individual or collective,
human or natural. But it is most clearly seen in his
relationship to the Wakonda Auga river, which inexorably erodes its banks, taking six inches each year
from everyone but the Stampers. The houses built by
early pioneers have been either swallowed by the river
or jacked up and moved back from its bank. More recent settlers have built homes a respectful distance
from the river. Yet the Stamper house remains on its
original site. Maintaining the shored-up jetty on which
the house rests is a constant, laborious struggle, and
this battle with the river is one which Hank, more than
any other Stamper, welcomes as a personal challenge.

An implicit parallel is drawn between Hank's defiance of the river and his opposition to the union
when he recalls how the river rose when he was ten
years old, undermined the bank, and drowned three
bobcat kittens he had adopted as pets. The passage is
interwoven with one in which the adult Hank loses a
new motorboat to the river and then sits, wet and
angry, listening to his lifelong adversary Floyd Evenwrite extol the virtues of the union. He decides that the
river, like the union, is "after some things I figured
belonged to me" and that "I aimed to do my best to
hinder it."

Hank's human adversaries are as various and
disparate in personality as the motives and weapons
they bring to bear in their battles with him. Jonathan
Bailey Draeger is, other than Lee, the most formidable.
He is a man of considerable intelligence, equanimity,
and cynicism, qualities which are ultimately thwarted
by the unparalleled stubbornness of Hank Stamper.

He considers himself a shrewd observer of human nature and is given to recording his observations as maxims in a notebook. Essentially a manipulator, he believes that the reactions of virtually all people can be codified and predicted. By the end of the novel, Draeger is forced to realize, as did Big Nurse, that some men are capable of acts of will which raise them above the foibles, weaknesses, and predictable behavior of the herd.

One of the primary thematic preoccupations of the novel lies in the tension between Draeger's articulate, essentially deterministic vision of humanity and Hank Stamper's roughly stated commitment to an existential view. Draeger, after observing innumerable supporting examples, believes that each man is no more than the predictable sum of the environmental and psychological forces acting upon him. Hank believes fervently in his own capacity to resist such forces, to make meaningful choices, and by acting upon them, to define himself.

Kesey's own philosophical bias here, as in *Cuckoo's Nest*, is clearly existential. The Stamper commitment, particularly in Hank and Henry (and ultimately in Lee), to individual courage, stoicism, and initiative against the forces of nature and collectivism make this obvious enough. Yet it is in the lapses from existential responsibility, the temptations to surrender one's individuality and capacity for resistance, that the main characters' ultimate existential choices are most clearly set off. The internal struggles of Hank and Lee are thus as significant to the novel's ultimate resolution as their conflict with one another. But before the climactic rendering of this theme through the major characters, Kesey illuminates the issue in a number of minor characters.

Arrayed most obviously with Draeger is a man decidedly unlike him, Floyd Evenwrite, the leader of the union local, whose personal insecurities and

resentments have as much to do with his anger toward
Hank as their ideological differences. Evenwrite is
programmed by psychological forces he does not
understand. His ambivalent feelings about his dead
father's failure as an idealistic union organizer for the
Industrial Workers of the World lead him to accept a
white-collar union job for which he is intellectually
and temperamentally unsuited. Confused and unhappy in this role, he is nonetheless incapable of free-
ing himself from it, and he vents his frustration
through an unreasoning hatred of Hank Stamper.

The character who is most clearly parallel in
temperament and method to Draeger is Teddy, the
soft, effeminate owner of the loggers' tavern, the Snag.
His internal monologues make clear his identification
with Draeger's quiet methods and confident, superior
intelligence. Only to the reader (and perhaps, implicitly, to Draeger) does Teddy reveal the contempt
in which he holds the blustering union men who attempt to conceal their fears through drink, bravado,
and the common sport of baiting Teddy. By hiding his
true feelings, Teddy has become quite successful in his
business; in his quiet manipulation of others, he is
similar to Draeger.

Throughout much of the novel, Lee is clearly
parallel to both Teddy and Draeger in his refusal to
fight Hank head-on, his attempt to win through
weakness, his reliance upon manipulation as a way of
life. It is only at the very end that Lee is able to relinquish the methods of Draeger and Teddy and adopt
the more honest approach of Hank.

A host of satellite figures fill out the gallery of
grotesques that populate the town of Wakonda. With
a far more subtle and comprehensive development of
character than in *Cuckoo's Nest*, Kesey presents with
understanding and some sympathy the backgrounds
and viewpoints of old Henry's contemporary and
rival, Boney Stokes; the obsequious Les Gibbons; the

bully, Big Newton; the ineffectual businessman, Willard Eggleston; and the prostitutes Simone and Indian Jenny. Each is given an in-depth treatment which mitigates the reader's distaste and illuminates each character's plight.

What these characters have in common is an inability to break out of the predetermined identity pressed upon them by external forces. Theirs is a deterministic view of life, one that contrasts strikingly with Hank's intensely existential drive to define himself through independent action. Big Newton, for example, is shown to be dominated by the expectations of his friends and relatives. Defined by his great size even to the point that it dictates his nickname, Big would find it difficult to become anything other than the sullen barroom brawler his fans expect him to be.

The tremendous pressures exerted by external forces to define a person are illuminated in the situation of Willard Eggleston, a "ridiculous little character . . . a cartoonist's wash-drawing of the capital-H henpecked husband. . . ." Willard has resisted being defined by his appearance, but "Now he knew better; if the book never opens up and comes out, it can be warped to fit the image others see. . . . No, a book wasn't invulnerable to the appearance of its cover. . . ." The concept of appearance dictating identity is explored in *Cuckoo's Nest* as well, when Bromden perceives the polarity between Harding, who has allowed his image in others' eyes to define him, and McMurphy, who has persisted in defining himself. Despite his awe at the difficulty of discovering one's identity, Bromden ultimately succeeds. Willard Eggleston's efforts are less successful. In an attempt to give meaning to his life, he goes to his death in an orchestrated auto "accident" which will provide his illegitimate son with insurance money.[4]

A further treatment of the appearance-identity concept informs the character of Hank's cousin Joby (who is further linked to Eggleston by the fact that their funerals occur on the same day). Until he was a teenager, Joby seemed destined because of his handsome face to follow in the image of his handsome, promiscuous, irresponsible father, Old Henry's brother Ben. But after being scarred permanently by a homely girl wielding a brush knife, Joby felt free to define himself as a kind, self-effacing, hardworking family man. In his cheerful acceptance of adversity and his deep and simple religious faith, Joby is similar to his Old Testament namesake, Job.

A further biblical parallel is suggested by the fact that after Joby drowns, pinned to the river bottom by a log that has fallen across his legs, Hank nails his jacket cuffs to the log in order not to lose the body when the tide goes out. Although the Christ imagery here is not part of an elaborate pattern as in *Cuckoo's Nest*, it is worth noting the pointed distinction in tone between the use of the image in connection with the profound loss represented by Joby's death and with the absurd flirtation with suicide by Lee in New Haven. In a parody of religious devotion, Lee must "kneel piously" to blow out the pilot light, while "the flame spewed symbolically from three jets, describing a fiery cross." In another cynically self-conscious biblical reference, Lee explains to his puzzled roommate, Peters, why he intends to return to Oregon: "to eat fatted calves." Lee is, indeed, a prodigal son returning. But the glib cleverness of his references to the Bible underline the differences between Lee and Joby. The former is self-indulgent and cynical, one with those who win through manipulation or weakness like Draeger, Teddy, or the hypochondriac Boney Stokes. Joby, though considerably less intelligent or imaginative, is a far more noble character in his honesty, devotion, and courage. After Joby's death, Lee must direct his intelligence and, more important, his *will* to replace Joby as Hank's brother.

Both biblical references and the appearance-identity pattern are developed further in terms of two minor but integral female characters, Indian Jenny and Simone, both of whom are evocatively and intelligently drawn. Indian Jenny is an aging prostitute obsessed with her rejection by Henry Stamper years ago. Comic but sympathetic in conception, she provides a link to the past, to Henry's youth; and it is in fact she who precipitates Henry's temporary metamorphosis back into the young logger he once was by threatening him with the power of the moon and thus reminding him of the dangerous tides on the day of the disastrous state park episode. Harmlessly witchlike, she is preoccupied with magical transformations. In her search for incantations she ties together such disparate supernatural visions as the Bible, the *Tibetan Book of the Dead*, and the *Classics Illustrated* version of *Macbeth*. Misled by its title, she buys Thomas Mann's *The Magic Mountain* and then discards it in disgust. Ultimately, she will return for her magic to the ancient rituals of her tribe.

In addition to providing comic relief and adding to the variety and depth of character in the novel, Jenny functions as a linking device, particularly to certain thematic and symbolic patterns which attach primarily to Lee. Her obsession with the magical properties of the full moon parallels Lee's, along with her search for incantations for purposes of vengeance, her immersion in both popular and high culture, and most specifically, her association with *Macbeth*, one of Lee's favorite sources of quotation and literary analogy. Finally, her decision to renounce the rituals of other cultures and return to her original heritage echoes Lee's more profound but similar decision to come to terms with his origins. Thus, this most unlikely of characters provides a sometimes humorous but always useful reiteration and illumination of Lee's progress toward self-knowledge.

The eclectic nature of Jenny's search for an icon
or talisman leads her to steal a plastic statue of Jesus
from the dashboard of a car belonging to Simone, a
character to whom she is linked by profession as well.
Like most of the inhabitants of Wakonda, Simone lives
within her own elaborate self-delusions. A plump,
pleasant woman, she is described primarily in terms of
food. She has "round, breadloaf shoulders" and a
mouth like a "dab of raspberry jam," and she is, upon
being deserted by her husband, a "muffin of misfor-
tune." Simone supports her children solely through her
regular activities as a party girl, yet she clings stead-
fastly to the notion, accepted by her clientele and the
town at large, that she is an amateur, in order to maintain her steadfast Catholicism. When this harmless
delusion is dispelled by the economic ripples of the WP
strike, Simone is traumatized both economically and
emotionally; like virtually everyone else in town, she
blames Hank Stamper for her problems.

Recognizing her prostitution for what it is,
Simone rejects it and embraces poverty and virtue. Yet
after a period of hunger and abstention, she comes to
realize that her haggard, ill-clothed appearance is
more disreputable in society's eyes than her former
vice. Comparing herself with Indian Jenny, she muses:
"I have become through virtue what that heathen slut
out there became through sin, a tramp, a shuffler in
dumpy dresses . . . to the women of the town I look
like the town whore."

After some indecision, Simone decides to return to
her former ways, but she does so with a cynicism that
was not characteristic of her before this experience.
Having come to a chilling realization of sin, she rejects
her religion and packs away her statue of the Virgin
Mary: "What good was such an idol to her now?
Could a virgin be expected to understand safety jelly?
or Listerine gargle? or . . . the cold, empty hollow left
when you for now and evermore relinquished

Virtue. . . . Don't make me laugh, Mary-doll. . . ."
As in McMurphy's influence on the characters of
Cuckoo's Nest, the truths revealed to the townspeople
by Hank Stamper's actions are not always welcome.
Some are strengthened, some hurt, some destroyed;
but virtually all are forced to come to terms with their
illusions, their preconceived *notions*.

If the surname "Stamper" suggests the boisterous,
violent, vital nature of his father's family, Leland
Stanford Stamper's given names reflect the gentility
and education of his mother. Yet both are connected
with the West, and it is there that Lee must travel in
order to discover his identity. In so doing, he repeats
the archetypally American journey of the entire
Stamper family, carried out over many generations.
His trip west completes a circle, bringing him back to
his origins to confront his past and learn who he is.

This journey ties Lee to his Stamper forbears, but
more specifically, it replicates the transworld circle
made by Hank after serving in the Marine Corps during the Korean War: "West, west, sailing out of San
Francisco west and after two years landing on the
eastern Seaboard, where his ancestors had first set
foot. He'd traveled in a straight line and completed a
circle." Arriving home, Hank realizes that he "was the
first of the Stampers to complete the full circle west."
Simply by taking a bus to Oregon, Lee has retraced the
physical journey of the Stampers and of Hank, the
quintessential Stamper. The emotional pilgrimage to
courage and self-knowledge will be a considerably
more difficult one.

This pilgrimage is illuminated by a thematic pattern which lies at the heart of Kesey's life as well as his
work: the confluence of popular and high culture. Lee
is characterized by a stilted, somewhat pretentious
tone of intellectuality in both his speech and the internal monologues which constitute much of the book's
narrative. He is given to literary allusions and ana-

logues from such sources as the Bible, Greek mythol-
ogy, and Shakespeare. Yet it is significant that he is
also steeped in the peculiar fantasies of popular culture, particularly movies and comic books.

In terms of classics, several examples present
themselves. Early in his stay in Oregon, he recounts to
his relatives the myth of the Greek giant Procrustes
with a "simple eloquence that he has never—even in
his dreams of teaching—imagined himself capable of."
Later, he envisions Goya's painting "Kronos Devour-
ing His Children" and recognizes "all the obvious
oedipal implications." But the primary source of Lee's
literary allusions is Shakespeare; and although there
are scattered references to other plays—Hank's teasing
of Henry is carried out in "sharper-than-a-serpent's-
tooth words," a reference to *King Lear*—most are to
Macbeth. Preoccupied with his problems, Lee finds
that the "innocent sleep would not come to knit up my
ravel'd sleeve of care." The first line of his letter to his
roommate, Peters, is "Good God, betimes the means
that makes us strangers!" Apologizing to Viv, he says,
"But as Lady Macbeth would say, 'The fit is momentary.' Regard me not." When the Stamper family flags
in its support of Hank, Lee observes that "The thanes
fly from us."

Lee is most clearly and profoundly similar to
Macbeth in his resolve to betray Hank, to "pull him
down" in order to supplant him. In this connection, he
writes Peters that "all I need do is screw my courage to
the sticking point." And, because his chosen mode of
vengeance is sexual and (as he will later reveal) he has
been impotent since his mother's suicide, he archly
wonders, "Do I hesitate . . . because simple old
masculinity doubts make me afraid to risk sticking my
courage to the screwing point?"

Throughout his often pretentious, sometimes self-
pitying association of himself with the tragic figure of
Macbeth, Lee's preoccupation is with besting Hank.

This concern informs his interest in popular culture as well. On the evening of his arrival in Oregon, ushered to his boyhood room, Lee finds a box of his old Captain Marvel comic books. In a lengthy digression, he recounts and rekindles his childhood (and lifetime) search for the magic word, his own "Shazam," which will transform him effortlessly, with a bolt of lightning, into an invincible hero. Eventually, he must learn what Bromden did: that no one is invulnerable, that hero worship is ultimately disappointing, and that courage and strength are not acquired from magical, external sources but nurtured within oneself in the long and difficult process of maturation.

For every hero in the scheme of this book, there is a monster. Thus, Lee sees himself as Jack climbing the beanstalk where Hank the giant awaits him. Old Henry, stamping about in his plaster leg cast, is like a "comic Frankenstein's monster." But Lee's most pervasive concern is with the werewolf motif, which recurs throughout the book, emphasizing the possibility that magical change can create a monster as well as a hero and introducing the function of the full moon as a totem, overseeing many of the major events of the novel. Both the moon and Lee's elusive "Shazam" function in the most dramatic sequences of the novel, at which time both are ultimately demythicized, stripped of their ostensible magic; but this comes much later, after Lee has painfully confronted many of his own hypocrisies and made several futile attempts to resolve his problems.

Another symbolic and thematic concern which grows out of Lee's interest in popular culture is the concept of imprisonment. In his room, Lee remembers that in his childhood

At night I used to imagine I was perishing in a hellish prison, condemned for deeds I had not done. And brother Hank was a trusty old turnkey, making his nightly rounds . . . as they did in all the Jimmy Cagney thrillers. . . . I fashion elaborate prison-break schemes . . . I—and Mother—tunnel to freedom beneath the river.

The prison motif is echoed by the bird cages owned by both Viv and Myra, which link them symbolically. Another physical prison is the cage in which Hank's bobcats drown. Fashioned, ironically, to protect them from the household dogs, it becomes their death trap. But freedom and imprisonment for the human characters are largely states of mind. It is significant that Viv first meets Hank when he is jailed by her uncle, a Colorado sheriff, and that in marrying her and taking her to Oregon, he frees her from the sterility and servitude of her life in Colorado, only to imprison her in his world. Hank is imprisoned by his own uncompromising commitment to strength and stoicism, his inability to admit weakness or sensitivity. Ultimately, each will break free of these limiting shackles; and even Lee gradually realizes that he must, like Viv and Hank, free himself from his past failures by an act of will.

Throughout his life, Lee has sought to avoid responsibility for coping with his own problems by blaming their origin on others. Yet, after three weeks in Oregon, surrounded by the unity of the family, he finds his anger waning. He momentarily takes a step into existential responsibility, rejecting the deterministic view he has hitherto held, that his childhood was traumatic and his adulthood neurotic because of other people: "Always before . . . I was able to fix the blame on some convenient villain: 'It was my brother Hank; it was my ancient fossil of a father; it was my mother . . . *they* were the ones who tore my young life asunder!' " In a dialogue with a full moon, Lee makes a decision.

So with the devil's-advocate moon grinning over my shoulder . . . with my stomach heavy with Viv's cooking and my head light with Hank's praise . . . I decided to bury the hatchet. I would blame my sad beginnings on no fiend but my own. . . . All those years barking various Shazams up the wrong tree—you'd think a foxy kid like me woulda known better. Magic words are too hard to come by, too tricky to pronounce, too unpredictable. Steady proper diet is the secret to growth.

This decision is described in terms of the choice between two types of metamorphosis. During their dialogue the moon has prompted Lee to think of the poem which is recited in virtually every Lon Chaney, Jr., "Wolfman" movie:

> Even a man who is pure of heart
> And says his prayers at night
> May turn to a wolf when the wolfbane blooms
> And the autumn moon is bright.

Lee has, significantly, rejected the fantasy of magical metamorphoses, whether into Captain Marvel or a werewolf. Instead, he decides to embrace with patience the natural process of maturation and growth as a human being. Intuitively following his emotions, he has rejected vengeance, the search for magical solutions to his problems, and the deterministic rationalization of his past in favor of an existential commitment to find and develop his identity. Yet his wounds are too deep, the temptation to seek easy redress too great, for the conversion to be completed this time. Later that same night, on a fox hunt, Lee has a falling-out with Hank and reverts to plans of vengeance, thoughts of finding his "Shazam." He is not yet able to stand as his own man, to fight back against his monster-hero brother and thus become his equal.

The choice to fight rather than run from life's problems is emphasized by a recurrent symbol pattern which is echoed in the novel's epigraph:

> Sometimes I get a great notion
> To jump into the river . . . an' drown.[5]*

Goodnight Irene. Words and Music by Huddie Ledbetter and John A. Lomax. TRO- © Copyright 1936 (renewed 1964) and 1950 (renewed 1978). Ludlow Music, Inc., New York, N.Y. Used by Permission.

The Wakonda Auga river represents for Henry and
Hank the adversary forces of nature to which they will
"never give a inch." One of Lee's earliest memories is
of Hank, training for swimming meets, swimming
tirelessly for hours into the current of the river without
making headway, an apparently Sisyphean activity
which nonetheless strengthened him for future vic-
tories. In a conversation during the fox hunt, Henry
relates a lengthy digression about the compulsion of
some animals to swim out to sea to certain death. In
the case of the pursued fox, a parable is implicitly
drawn to human life, in which Lee is identified with
the fox, who must choose whether to run, or swim, or
"turn an' fight." Again, Hank, immediately before his
brutal barroom brawl with Big Newton, thinks silently
of the lesson he hopes his brother will learn: "But you
see, Lee? I ain't running out to sea from him, I don't
give a shit how big he is: he can whip my ass but he
can't run me out to sea!"

Henry's tales of swimming animals underline
Lee's early preoccupation with suicide. As in *Cuckoo's
Nest*, suicide is a recurrent motif here, primarily
significant in terms of Myra's death and Lee's comi-
cally unsuccessful attempt early in the book. The concept is echoed in Willard Eggleston's death and
Draeger's observation that "this area has two or three
natives a month take that one-way dip." Again, the
polarity between those characters who fight and those
who choose to give up and drown is emphasized. Ultimately, Lee will take Hank's lesson to heart and,
standing with the river at his back, turn and fight for
the first time in his life.

Even more than *Cuckoo's Nest*, *Notion* is rich in
animal imagery. Many of the characters are defined in
animal terms. Thus, Big Newton is the "Nemean
Lion," Teddy a "Teddybear," Joby's wife Jan a
"lamb," cousin Andy "like a bear," the town wives a
"bunch of heifers," and so on. More pervasive still are

the numerous bird images used by Kesey. Old Henry is, in his various moods, "modest as a turkey gobbler," "hawklike," a "woodpecker," a "peacock," and a "broken gull." Jan is a "swan," Lee "deadpan as an owl," Joby a "rooster," and Simone a "chicken." As in *Cuckoo's Nest*, the mindless cruelty of the group to the individual is associated with the pecking of hens. Like McMurphy, Hank uses the metaphor to describe the town wives, a "bunch of hens" who "peck at" Viv. The recurrent association with bird images will later be seen to link Viv and Myra.

Finally, another echo of *Cuckoo's Nest* is found in the attachment to Hank of the Canada honker, and particularly of a lone goose, lost in the fog. Hank describes its call: "not exactly afraid. . . . Different. Almost human. . . . *Where is my world?* he was wanting to know, *and where the hell am I if I can't locate it?* . . . like me. . . . Only with me, I couldn't figure what I thought I'd lost. . . ." Hank, like McMurphy, shares with the Canada honker the strength and pride to go his own way, to defy human attempts to destroy or capture him. But, like this particular goose, Hank has at this point lost his way. The passage appears shortly before he loses Joby, Henry, Viv, and, temporarily, his determination. Hank spares the life of the lost goose by telling Joby not to shoot it. Similarly, Hank, lost in a spiritual fog when his previously confident conceptions of his world seem less applicable in terms of Lee, will escape the death which claims Henry and Joby. Like the goose, he will have the opportunity to find his difficult way out of the fog.

The fox hunt establishes an effective symbol cluster in which Hank is implicitly identified with the courageous dog, Molly, who strikes out alone to track a bear while the other dogs choose the safer course of clinging together in a pack (like the union men and the townspeople), and Lee is associated with the cunning

fox. Significantly, Molly is mortally wounded, not by
the bear but by a snake which bites her in the hind-
quarters without warning. The implication that Hank
cannot be beaten by head-on opposition but only by
treachery is reinforced by Kesey's use of the snake
as metaphor at other points (e.g., the fawning,
treacherous Les Gibbons has a "tongue pink and quick
as a snake's").

During the hunt, Kesey again skillfully weaves
several temporal planes, presenting subplots simultaneously with the main plot. While Hank and Joby
follow the dogs, Lee surreptitiously strokes Viv's neck
with his hand. As he attempts this first sexual overture,
using a foxlike cunning rather than courage to oppose
Hank, Henry relates a bawdy story about a fox's sexual
pursuit of Hank's young bluetick bitch years before.
The parallel to Lee's pursuit of Viv is obvious. A more
striking aspect of the scene, however, is Kesey's insis-
tent focus on Lee's hand, "coming once more to life,"
caressing Viv's throat in the dark as she recognizes her
ambivalence toward the contact.

As in *One Flew Over the Cuckoo's Nest*, hands are
indexes of character.[6] When Hank and Lee meet again
after twelve years apart, they find themselves unable
to shake hands. The fact that Hank has lost two fingers
in a logging accident during that time and that consequently his swimming form is slightly clumsier is seen
by Lee as an indication that Hank may now be "pulled
down" more easily. During the first day on the job,
Hank lends Lee his gloves so that Lee's soft hands are
protected from damage, while Hank absorbs more cuts
and scrapes. Later Lee remarks upon his own develop-
ing calluses as an indication of his acclimation to
physical work; and on the fox hunt, Viv feels on her
throat his "fingers thin and soft beneath the new shell
of calluses." Simone's is a "dimpled, baby's hand,"
Viv's hands are "slender, flickering," Draeger's are
"groomed, like two pompous and pedigreed show-
dogs," and Evenwrite's are "knotted and ugly, like

mongrels made all red and hairless with mange." In moving from manual logging work to a white-collar union position, Evenwrite has lost his calluses. As a result, his hands "barely felt like his own. They felt naked, and nervous, and like somebody else's hands. No calluses was how come." In taking his new position, Evenwrite has lost his sense of identity.

The anthropomorphic quality of the natural forces opposing the Stampers is emphasized in a passage in which clouds are "like clawed hands thrust grasping up . . . like the hands of something trapped and determined to claw its way up on land, or pull the land down beneath the sea." Again, the tree which, in falling, traps Joby and tears Henry's arm off, wounding him fatally, hits Hank like "a swinging green fist."

Both Lee and Hank are forced to come to terms with painful realizations as a result of the fatal episode in the state park. The defection of less committed relatives from the logging effort leaves Hank, Joby, and the partially disabled Henry struggling to meet their deadline under difficult and dangerous circumstances, cutting enormous trees in the virgin wilderness without the aid of modern machinery. Indian Jenny has attempted to frighten Henry with portentous threats of the moon's mystical power. Although he laughs at the superstitious overtones, the threat reminds Henry of the particularly dangerous tides to be expected because of the full moon; and the tide, despite Henry's awareness of it, contributes to the logging accident. The moon is, thus, shown to be a potent natural force whose significance to the novel's symbolic structure is reinforced at the same time that it is divested of its supernatural, magical aura, just as Lee's search for a magic word will be deglamorized later that night as an indirect result of the same episode.

With Indian Jenny's warning spurring him only to greater effort, old Henry becomes rejuvenated. The narrative shifts to his point of view, and he becomes a more dynamic figure. Hank feels that the "cast had broken to reveal a younger and at the same time more mature person," an image which echoes the metamorphosis pattern which has hitherto focused primarily on Lee.

It is fitting that Henry should momentarily regain the spirit of his youth and take over the leadership of the logging operation, which Hank relinquishes to him gladly and with unconcealed admiration, for in the state park the trees are as massive and the legally permissible mechanical aids as primitive as those of nineteenth-century logging. The work is, in effect, a trip into the past, into Henry's youth, into the history of the Stampers and the country. The results are both as exhilarating and as terrifying as anything that befell the loggers of the previous century in their struggles to make a life and a living in the forest.

In the excitement of dangerous work against an impending deadline, Joby adopts aloud the Stamper battle cry: "Don't give a inch!" and the three men become "an efficient, skilled team . . . almost one man." The fusion of the three clearly prefigures the more profound and significant fusion of Lee and Hank at the novel's conclusion and indicates the potential both for success and disaster inherent in the task of driving the logs down the river.

It is during this scene that Hank himself becomes guilty of a lapse from strength and responsibility. Emotionally and physically overdrawn, he gladly accepts Henry's assumption of leadership. He thinks: *"You run it. I'm tired rassling it. . . . Me, just turn me on and aim me . . . I'm tired, but I'll work. If you take over."* He has, in his exhaustion, abdicated his responsibility to lead, to think as a human being. Instead, he is satisfied to drive himself like a machine under another's directions. He is, in fact, described in mechanical terms during this scene. He works "mechanically," "relentless as a machine," and his arms are "cable-strong."

With Hank's lapse from existential responsibility, the state park sequence comes closer to a naturalistic vision than anything Kesey has previously written. Working like machines, the men "mesh" with one another and momentarily lose their individual identities. Dwarfed by the trees they seek to bring down, they are thwarted by natural forces stronger than they: the moon and its tides, the combination of gravity and unpredictable winds, and finally, the log which crushes two of them and leaves Hank apparently defeated. Hank's reaction to Joby's death emphasizes nature's indifference.[7] He stares at the "surface of water that lay featureless and unruffled over Joe. No different from any of the rest of the surface, all the way across the river, all the way out to sea. *(But Joe Ben is dead, don't you realize?).*" In retrospect, Hank recognizes his failure and accepts responsibility for it:

Yeah, a fellow can look back and add up all the reasons and say, "Well, it ain't really so hard to figure how come I was so punchy and so logy and so careless out working the state park . . . what with all the hassles banging at me so long. . . ." But just the same, being able to look back and give reasons and all that still don't do much toward making a man proud of what happened because of them reasons. Not if he can look back as well and see how he . . . by god *should* have kept it from happening. There's shames a man can never reason away. . . .

Ultimately, it will be this capacity for honesty, this refusal to rationalize, this willingness to accept the responsibility for his own actions that will bring Hank back from his lapse into—or rather, his brief flirtation with—determinism, into meaningful action once again.

In a passage of unremittent pain, Hank helplessly witnesses Joby's death, leaves his dying father at the hospital, is viciously beaten by three thugs hired by Evenwrite, returns home to find the boat gone, and swims across the river with his last measure of strength to find Viv and Lee in a postcoital embrace. As Hank

vomits before passing out, Lee cruelly repeats what he
sees as an "incantation," a long-remembered sarcastic
remark made to the twelve-year-old Lee on the day he
and Myra left Oregon: "Musta been somethin godawful rich to make you so godawful sick." Lee has
found his "Shazam," but the result is disappointing:

I knew that I had in no way achieved the stature I had subconsciously dreamed that my revenge would bring about. I
had very successfully completed my ritual of vengeance; I
had accurately mouthed all the right mystical words . . . but
instead of turning myself into a Captain Marvel . . . I had
merely created another Billy Batson.

Lee's search for a magic word has been deglamorized,
robbed of its mystical potential, much as Indian
Jenny's invocation of the moon has been.

　　This scene underlines a central thematic concern
of Kesey's work. In *Cuckoo's Nest*, McMurphy draws a
clear distinction between those people who win vic-
tories fairly through making themselves stronger and
those "ball-cutters" who win only by making their
adversaries weaker. Throughout most of his stay in
Oregon, Lee has given up any hope of "measuring up"
to Hank and has chosen to work instead at "pulling
him down." Although he has succeeded briefly in doing so, the victory is tasteless and unrewarding. It is at
this point that Lee begins to realize that he can never
achieve a satisfactory victory over Hank and the personal demons he represents until he has confronted his
own fear and weakness and developed his own courage
and strength.

　　After Joby's death, Hank looks back over his life
wearily, slipping for the moment into the resigned
determinism which hitherto has been associated with
Lee and the townspeople.

And yet . . . above that ballooning sense of loss that you
always feel right after somebody close dies . . . I experienced
a sort of feeling of *relief*. I was tired, and it was almost

over. . . . Finally finished. After going on now for Christ
how long? . . . since . . . this morning. . . . No. Before
that. . . . Since Joby first got me out for football and made
me his hero. . . . Since the old man nailed that plaque on my
wall. . . . Since, since, since. . . .

In his exhaustion, Hank comes to a painful recognition
of his own capacity for weakness and relinquishes the
belief that anyone can be absolute and unfaltering in
his strength: "No, there ain't any true strength; there's
just different degrees of weakness. . . ." Hank has
finally learned that everyone must sometimes give
an inch.

Hank falters for a few days. Almost meek after
the accident and Lee's adulterous vengeance, he gives
up the hope of fulfilling the contract with Wakonda
Pacific, accepts an invitation for drinks from Floyd
Evenwrite, and determines to seek the path of least
resistance with Lee until the latter's departure. During
this period, the reactions of the union members and
the other townspeople are curiously similar to those of
the inmates of *Cuckoo's Nest* when McMurphy learns
to be cagey. Although they purport to be pleased, they
are frightened and irritable, bickering among one
another. Teddy notes a paradoxical increase in their
liquor consumption. Clearly, they are ambivalent
about the loss of an adversary of Hank's stature. The
phenomenon is clarified by a symbol pattern in which
Hank is identified with a tall tree.

The association is established quite early, when
Lee describes Hank "diving into the river, naked and
white and hard as a peeled tree." Later, referring to
Hank, Lee resolves that "I needed to fell the tree that
had been hogging my sunshine before I even ger-
minated." Just as the Canada honker rises above other
birds in the symbolic scheme of Kesey's novels and
Hank rises above other men, so "over all these other
plants, like a higher order of plant life, stood the fir—
filling the sky with towering peaks." At one point,

Joby looks out over a landscape of felled trees and remarks "How Them Mighty Are Fallen." He goes on to articulate the phenomenon of "people likin' to watch the trees come down . . . a natural hell-driven desire to see the righteous fallen." But it is Hank who makes it clear that it is not the righteous so much as the mighty that people like to see toppled: "They'd come for miles to see somebody chop down that tallest-tree-in-the-state up yonder in Astoria. . . . Nope . . . it ain't the righteous, it ain't that. . . ."

Thus, his adversaries watch expectantly for Hank to be felled; yet once he appears to be, they are unhappy and disappointed. Floyd Evenwrite is "Amazed and, he found, a little disappointed: he'd expected more of Hank. And he felt that Hank had betrayed him." And "Even Biggy Newton . . . pledged to the last ounce of his stunted intelligence as Hank Stamper's arch enemy, found himself feeling less and less overjoyed. As he got drunker and drunker in the Snag."

It is, ironically, Lee who revives Hank's anger and determination and helps bring his brother and himself to a new and more striking commitment to existential action. When Lee returns briefly to the Stamper house on Thanksgiving Day, he attempts for the last time to win through weakness, taunting Hank into a fight in the hope that Viv, in sympathy, will leave Oregon with him. Hank learns that the recognition of his capacity for weakness need not preclude the ability to choose strength. He accepts his responsibility to make moral choices, to act upon them, and by so doing, to define himself. And Lee, amazed, finds himself fighting back. He too chooses courage and action over passive weakness.

Throughout the novel, Hank and Lee have loved Viv and fought over her but have not recognized her human needs. As Kesey remarked in retrospect in 1972,

Women's Lib was the real issue in *Notion*. I didn't know this when I wrote it, but think about it: It's about men matching egos and wills on the battleground of Vivian's unconsulted hide. When she leaves at the end of the book, she chooses to leave the only people she loves for a bleak and uncertain but at least *equal* future.[8]

The reader's awareness of Viv's significance is heightened by a dramatic device by which Lee is introduced to her in gradual stages. In his room on the first night home, Lee hears Viv sing. Her voice is the "succulent warbling of a rare fairyland bird," and she is singing a lullaby, to which he falls asleep. Later, upon awakening, he spies upon Viv's empty sewing room (formerly his mother's) through the peephole which had revealed his mother's affair with Hank, and he realizes by its furnishings that "Hank has an exceptional woman for a wife." The next day, in the woods, Lee eats the excellent lunch packed by Viv, the "girl he had yet to meet but who was constantly growing in stature in his estimation." That evening, Lee again looks through the hole between rooms, and sees Viv herself:

I remember perfectly my first impression: that the girl—not the lamp behind her—was emitting the light. She stood there, motionless, her back to me . . . quite pale, quite slender, with wonderfully long sorrel-blond hair . . . and she made me think of a burning candle. . . . Then she turned, and as she walked directly toward my spying eyes . . . I saw that her cheeks were wet with crying.

When Lee finally meets Viv, he finds her "as lovely in the hard kitchen light as she had been in the mellow glow of her room."

There is, in fact, virtually nothing about Viv that is not attractive and admirable. Even her name suggests aspects of her personality: she is vivacious, vivid, full of life. Yet Viv is imprisoned by Hank in his world. Despite their mutual love, Viv's life as Hank's wife is in some respects similar to Myra's life with Henry and

Hank. Several symbolic patterns point up this parallel.

Viv is associated with birds on several occasions. Her voice sounds to Lee like a "rich bird-note"; she wishes she could fly through the forest, "skimming through it inches above the ground . . . like the wren. . . ." But she is most clearly associated with the canary, which is one of the two requests she makes of Hank before marrying him. After it dies, the empty cage remains in her room, "about as birdless as a cage can get, she thinks."

Each of these associations ties Viv symbolically to Myra, who "was dark-haired and slight . . . like some kind of funny bird. . . ." When Myra and Lee leave Oregon, the boat is loaded with "bundles, *birdcages*, hatboxes," while the "woman stands watching, thin *bird* hand resting on the shoulder of her twelve-year old son, who leans against her hip, polishing his eyeglasses with the hem of her *canary-yellow* skirt." [My italics]

The empty bird cages of Viv and Myra point up the emptiness of their lives and the sense of imprisonment within them that both feel. The parallels between Myra and Viv are not absolute. Although Viv is well-read, she is neither urbane nor highly educated. Although sensitive, she is not brittle and neurotic like Myra. Yet Hank and Lee persist in imposing further similarities upon Viv. Although Viv's hair is sorrel-blond and Myra's dark, Hank repeatedly jokes with her about dying it black. Her second premarital request of Hank was to be for a short haircut, but Hank is adamant in his preference for long hair:

". . . I like you better with it all hanging and swinging."

"But it gets in the way . . . and gets so dirty—"

"Well then, maybe we'll just have to dye it black." He laughed. . . . So she never made the second request.

Again, when Viv is pregnant with Hank's child, before her miscarriage, Hank introduces the same "joke":

"I wonder—what would it be like, black?"
    "The baby?"
    "No, no." He laughed. "Your hair."

Just as Hank is preoccupied with replicating Myra
in Viv, Lee attempts to repay, in his incestuous relationship with his brother's wife, the injury done him by his
brother and mother. The attempt brings into focus the
elaborate pattern of vaguely incestuous relationships
which link the characters by analogy. Myra was seduced by Henry, who was old enough to be her father.
Hank was seduced by Myra, his stepmother. The central conflict between Hank and Lee is Oedipal; and
Hank has been like a father to Lee, not merely in his
sexual relationship with Myra but in the repeated instances in which (as Lee gradually realizes) Hank took
on responsibility for his younger brother. Thus, in
sleeping with Viv, Lee commits incest on two levels.
First, he has bedded the wife of his symbolic father;
and second, insofar as Viv represents Myra for Lee as
much as for Hank, he has repossessed his mother sexually, apparently resolving his own classically Oedipal
conflict, although the resolution will ultimately be
seen as a false, unsatisfactory one.
    The incestuous parallels among the principal
characters suggest certain further parallels between
Hank and Lee, who, despite their obvious differences
and antipathies, share certain similarities. Both have
lost their mothers at an early age, Hank to death and
Lee to Hank. They share the same father and, briefly,
the same wife, Viv. Lee's early, cold-blooded vision of
Viv as "my weapon" against Hank quickly gives way
to love for her; yet the plan to dehumanize Viv, to use
her as a tool, prefigures Viv's realization that she has
not been allowed to develop her identity. Unlike
Myra, she will ultimately leave Hank and Lee on her
own terms, with the determination to create a viable,
individual future for herself.
    In a very real sense, Myra is a pervasive ghost

throughout the novel. The extent to which she looms over Viv's relationships with both Hank and Lee is rendered clearly by means of a subtle device. Searching the Stamper attic for an insurance policy before leaving for the East, Lee discovers a "photograph of Viv seated beside a small bespectacled boy. The child, about five or six—one of the up-and-coming young Stampers, I surmised—glowered solemnly in the direction of the photographer's telltale shadow." It is only when Viv, seated in the Snag waiting for her bus, looks at the picture later that day that we understand from her reaction that it is in fact a picture of Myra and Lee: "For this woman, this dead image, she feels a hatred that sings in her ears like steam. This woman has been like a dark fire that melted them all almost beyond recognition."

Lee's misapprehension of the picture's subject strikingly indicates the degree to which he has found in Viv not herself but the ghost of Myra. Just as the shadow of the photographer (possibly Hank) falls over him in the photograph, while his mother smiles and he glowers, Myra's shadow falls over both Lee's and Hank's relationship with Viv. The fact that he does not recognize himself as a child suggests further the search for identity which he has not yet completed; and his description of the child as "one of the up-and-coming young Stampers" is ironically accurate, for Lee is indeed a Stamper, deny it how he will.

A similar crisis of identity has earlier occurred to Hank when, awakening in the night, he is terrified by the sight in a window of a face, "wide-eyed, wild-haired, with a mouth twisted in horror." It is, of course, his own reflection, but the horror of it and his momentary inability to recognize it indicate his current emotional state of flux and the fact that he must define himself anew.

Both Hank and Lee ultimately accept the painful responsibility to develop more fully as human beings by changing their preconceived notions of themselves. Viv has learned this before either brother. Insofar as mirror images suggest the perception of one's identity, Viv is associated with them at two major points of change in her life. Before leaving Colorado behind for her new life with Hank, she bids a ritualistic farewell to her childhood possessions and to the child she was, and "chiding herself for being such a silly, kissed the face in the glass goodbye." In a parallel situation, torn between Lee and Hank before she has made her decision to leave Oregon, she feels "like a small child. And becomes aware of her image once more, vaguely reflected in the dirty attic window: what does it mean, all this concern about our images?"

Momentarily confused and childlike, Viv is nonetheless more flexible than Lee or Hank, more willing to adolesce into a new stage of adult development. Rejecting preconceptions and vague images, she clearly recognizes Lee and Myra in the photograph, recognizes Hank's problem and her own responsibility to herself. Sitting in the Snag with the photo album, Viv "hears Hank now for the first time, trying to tell her, and Lee, finally hears them, and sees for herself how they had all been cheated." She knows that "I love them but I cannot give myself for them. Not my whole self. I have no right to do that."

In short, Viv knows now what Lee has just learned and silently articulated in one of the most evocative passages in the novel:

For there is always a sanctuary more, a door that can never be forced, whatever the force, a last, inviolable stronghold that can never be taken, whatever the attack; your vote can be taken, your name, your innards, even your life, but that last stronghold can only be surrendered. And to surrender it for any reason other than love is to surrender love. Hank had always known this without knowing it and by making him doubt it briefly I had made it possible for both of us to discover it. I knew it now. And I knew that to win my love, my life, I would have to win back for myself the right to this last stronghold.

Which meant winning back the strength I had bartered away years ago for a watered-down love.

Which meant winning back the pride I had exchanged for pity.

Which meant not letting that bastard make that run against the river without me, not again, not this time; even if we both drowned, I did not intend to spend another dozen years in his shadow, no matter how big it loomed!

Lee runs toward his brother, leaving behind Viv, his bus ticket, and his packet of old letters and photographs. Viv picks up the ticket, cuts her hair short with a borrowed knife, and boards the eastbound bus. As she passes them, she sees "two tiny figures leaping foolishly from log to log." In cutting her hair free, Viv has cut herself free from others' conceptions of her. In leaving Oregon, she sets out to find her own, independent future, to define her own destiny. Her action, coming from the apparently docile woman she has hitherto been, looms as large and startling as the slamming of the door by Ibsen's Nora in *A Doll's House*.

And Lee and Hank, the "tiny," "foolish" figures, seek to define theirs. Like McMurphy, they believe that the struggle itself is more important than the result. Like him, they may not be able to overcome the massive forces against them: the unwieldy weight of the logs and that of the union and the society that has spawned it. Like him, they may ultimately be destroyed but never defeated. It is fitting that the novel close here, with Viv, Hank, and Lee each at the beginning of a journey and not its end, for it is the essence of their vision and Kesey's that the constant potential for new beginnings is central to the dynamic process that is human life.

5

Kesey's Garage Sale:
Advertisements
for Himself

Kesey's Garage Sale is strikingly analogous to Norman Mailer's *Advertisements for Myself* (1959). Each is an unorthodox collection of fragments, interviews, and other short pieces published by a talented, notorious novelist in his thirties during a lengthy lapse between novels. More important, each is given unity and focus through the author's candid statements about his evolving attitude toward his art.

A good example occurs in "An Impolite Interview with Ken Kesey," in which Kesey tells Paul Krassner, "I feel my personal energies swinging back to writing." Shortly thereafter, he explains that unfortunately his public statements, even on subjects in which he has no true expertise, carry "a disproportionate weight" and that in order to avoid making irresponsible or unqualified pronouncements he has determined to "shut my mouth and the door to my writing room and finish [another novel] and answer out of my range no more. Passing off what-might-be-true as fiction seems a better vocation to me than passing off what-is-quite-possibly-fiction as truth." The pointed implication that the role of public figure, even within a subculture, has been a false and disappointing one suggests a new stage of maturity for Kesey; and the vow to concentrate on a new novel presents an attractive prospect for his readers.

Although the artistic value of *Kesey's Garage Sale* is limited, bits of information useful to the student of Kesey's work are strewn throughout the volume. For example, in a section entitled "Who Flew Over What?" Kesey answers several questions about the composition of *Cuckoo's Nest*:

Yes, McMurphy was fictional, inspired by the tragic longing of the real men I worked with on the ward, the sketches of whom, both visual and verbal, came more easily to my hand than anything before or since, and those sketches gradually enclosed for me the outline of the hero they wanted.

And, yes, I did write the book both on the ward and on drugs, double-checking my material so to speak.

This section also includes Kesey's drawings of McMurphy, Bromden, and the other patients.

Kesey tangentially provides further insights into the influences upon his first two novels when he discusses other novelists in a section entitled "Tools from My Chest," originally published in *The Last Supplement to the Whole Earth Catalog*. Of Hemingway, he says:

Sometimes its [sic] hard to tell if Hemingway was writing the Judy Garland story or if it was Janis Joplin writing the Ernest Hemingway story; they're all such tragically similar tales of what happens to people who stare a trace too long into the Spotlight . . . don't be misled by the bodies of bullfighters or the riddled remains of soldiers; look instead for live trout on the bottom vibrating against the clean current, or bacon fat going cold on a veteran's breakfast plate, or old boards going sharp into focus through a pair of binoculars; in those delicate transitions where nothing actually moves you may find something of the slow and gentle old giant.

In the clear and compassionate perception of the damage done Hemingway's talent by his fame, one can see Kesey's awareness of this pitfall and his determination to avoid it. The statement of what Kesey finds most evocative in Hemingway's fiction illuminates for the reader of *Cuckoo's Nest* and *Notion*

obvious parallels—the clarity of images, the precise attention to small but significant details—between the
work of the two writers.

Other writers, more contemporary to Kesey,
whom he mentions with admiration are William Bur-
roughs ("the only writer that had really done anything
new with writing since Shakespeare") and Larry
McMurtry ("a beautiful writer"). Nonetheless, Kesey
can still say, "Faulkner is my favorite," and go on to
write a brief appreciation in mild parody of Faulkner's
style. It seems clear that *Notion*, in its shifting point of
view and frequent stream-of-consciousness passages,
and *Cuckoo's Nest*, told not by an idiot but by a man
quite as alienated from his surroundings, are both indebted to *The Sound and the Fury*.

As I have indicated earlier, the primary value of
Garage Sale lies in Kesey's screenplay, "Over the
Border." Arthur Miller, in his intelligent, measured introduction to *Garage Sale*, emphasizes this. Primarily
positive in his assessment of the collection and the era
and "movement" of which it is symptomatic, Miller
nonetheless recognizes its weaknesses and limitations.
He begins by admitting that "This is, of course, a
chaotic volume, and cynics will easily dispose of it as a
transparent attempt to capitalize on twice-published
material, plus stuff lying at the bottom of the drawer."
He points out that critics "will have to notice pages of
mawkishness, self-conscious letter-writing you might
call it," but insists that "it finally does achieve a certain dignity and courage, and these may count for
more in the end than its weaknesses." Miller goes on to
state that "this book and the movement it voices . . .
at its best was and is a redemptive thrust. . . . The
proof lies in Kesey's screenplay above all, I think."

Again, focusing on the importance of "Over the
Border," Miller states that "this book is a sort of
geologic section of some fifteen years in the wilderness,
but all jumbled together . . . culminating in his

screenplay, from whose final pages you can look down
as from a height and begin to sense a form at last in the
whole insane pageant." "Over the Border" is in-
disputably central to *Kesey's Garage Sale* and to the
insight it provides into the development of Kesey's
mind and art since the writing of *Notion*; and it is the
remarkable conclusion to the screenplay that most
lends it its significance. But this conclusion can be best
understood after a brief plot summary and a discussion of the technical devices and narrative methods
employed by Kesey.

Arrested, in the company of Behema (a minor) for
possession of marijuana, Devlin Deboree counterfeits
his suicide and then flees to Mexico to avoid prosecution. As a fugitive, he lives in a state of paranoia. He
soon is joined by his followers, the Animal Friends, including his wife Betsy, his children Caleb, Quiston,
and Sherree, and the pregnant Behema, who travel to
Mexico in a 1939 International Harvester school bus
driven by "Sir Speed" Houlihan. Other characters include Claude and Blanche Muddle, Rex May, Sandy
Pawku, Mickey Write, Rampage, Undine Reyes,
M'Kehla, and THE VOICE IN THE SKY.

In Mexico, they have various adventures, including Deboree's escape by freight train from Mexican Federales, and conduct experiments with hallucinogenic drugs. These culminate in a mass LSD trip
at the seashore. Deboree's delusions of grandeur have
grown to the point where he is convinced that he can
command lightning bolts by the power of his mind.
His arrogant negligence results in the drowning death
of his son Quiston. But the Animal Friends, in a strikingly effective, surrealistic passage, reveal themselves
as gods. After much debate, they mercifully reverse
time to give Deboree another chance to redeem himself. Deboree rescues his son and in the aftermath is
left to ponder his lesson and seek a new path to a more
humble sense of self at the conclusion of the screenplay.

In subject matter, the movement of "Over the

Border" is from the recognizably autobiographical[1] to the fictional and fantastic. In vision, it is from the pedestrian to the mystical. In technique, it is from the conventionally cinematic to the experimental. As Kesey proceeds from an essentially uninspired recounting of his experiences to an incisive and candid revelation of his failures, the devices he uses become more experimental, bizarre, and effective.

Early in the screenplay, he employs such standard cinematic effects as credits presented over opening scenes and such useful but common dramatic tools as interior monologues. Shortly thereafter, Deboree communicates with the Animal Friends by sending them a tape recording from his hideout in Mexico, and "Deboree's Voice" alternates with the comments of his listening family and friends. When the voice begins to speak in a rapid, high-pitched manner, reflecting Deboree's growing paranoia and nervousness, a logical mechanical explanation is provided:

SANDY PAWKU: Why is his voice getting higher and faster?
GRIP: The batteries were running down on his machine as he taped this, making the tape go slower and slower, thereby getting more words to the inch . . . then, when we play it back at the regular speed, those words come by faster and faster, . . .

This rooting in concrete reality extends, at first, to other devices and situations. When Deboree is fearful of being captured by Mexican police under circumstances disturbingly parallel to those of his American arrest, he remarks: "Cops below again and me trapped on the roof again. Oh misguided me! I'm caught in a film loop. . . ." The situation, and Deboree's perception of it, are presented not in arch, surrealistic terms but merely in terms of conventional dramatic irony; and the expression "I'm caught in a film loop," which might have tempted Kesey into an experimental technique, remains no more than an effective metaphor.

Although Kesey provides an omniscient narrator, referred to portentously enough as "VOICE IN THE SKY," its function throughout much of the screenplay is no more godlike, mystical, or experimental than that of the Stage Manager in Thornton Wilder's *Our Town* or the Chorus in Shakespeare's *Henry V*. Later, when Mickey Write presents his point of view through the hackneyed device of a journal, the only unusual thing about it is that it is reproduced in holograph, a reminder that the screenplay is meant to be viewed (whether on screen or page) with the cinematic advantage of the close-up. Further visual additions appear on each page, in the form of drawings, cartoons, and puzzles, reminiscent in style of such underground comics as those of R. Crumb, which fill the margins and sometimes are superimposed over the text. The puckish, pop-culture tone of this form is emphasized by the inclusion of an entry blank for a contest offering prizes for the best coloring job on one or more pages of the screenplay.

As the screenplay progresses, techniques reminiscent of the hallucinatory, subjective narrative of *Cuckoo's Nest* and the temporal experimentation of *Notion* are brought into play. Deboree, in Mexico, and the Animal Friends, in the United States, each take LSD and begin *"drifting bodiless among the stars in a languid circle."* In a scene which grows integrally out of the earlier, realistic scene with the tape recorder, they speak to one another, Deboree answering their questions in a dialogue. During this scene, time loses its impenetrable rigidity, as in *Notion*, and "Sir Speed" Houlihan says: "Now, let's say it isn't Easter 1965. Let's say it's . . . 1972 . . . and I've been dead a couple of years. . . ." He goes on, in an aside to Behema, to describe in detail the circumstances of Neal Cassady's actual death (in 1968) and then to quote a 1972 article in *Playboy* in which he was tangentially referred to as a psychopath. He asks Deboree to avenge this slight; and as both author and reader are aware, the passage archly achieves that very effect. Kesey would later publish a moving tribute to Cassady in the semifictional memoir "The Day After Superman Died" in the October 1979 issue of Esquire.[2]

Late in the screenplay, Deboree recounts his escape from five Mexican Federales to his followers and his admiring older son, Quiston. He describes the police in terms of cartoon animals: "They looked like five forest animals from a very . . . *low-rent* forest. . . ." As he speaks,

Quiston's faraway expression dissolves into scene around the bus. . . . Things are a bit different, enhanced by the influence of Quiston's visualization. The bus is in better condition with new tires on mag wheels, shiny chrome and a wriggling Jackson Pollock finish. . . . Also, Houlihan, Rampage and Mickey are somewhat shorter while Quiston's father has become taller and more heroic of stance. But the most striking difference is the appearance of the five Federales . . . they are all animated cartoon caricatures superimposed onto the real picture a la Disney. . . .

Thus, the scene embodies the techniques not only of cinema but of the animated cartoon form. The palpable subjectivity of Quiston's perception is akin to that of Bromden, a parallel which is reinforced by the metaphor of physical stature, when he pictures his father as taller than the others. The cartoon character vision is similar to that experienced by Bromden when, at Harding's description of the inmates as rabbits, he "sees" them turn into Disney-like bunnies. Here Kesey has begun to demonstrate the strengths and versatility of the form within which he is operating, by employing techniques of drama, cinema, and fiction. The obvious concern with autobiographical experience begins to be overshadowed by artistic effects similar to those of the two novels.

The conclusion of "Over the Border" is rich in technique and thematic statement. For the communal

acid trip staged to demonstrate his putative power
over lightning, Deboree appears dramatically costumed, "absolutely astonishing in an all-white outfit:
white boots, white tights, belt and shirt . . . topped
by a white satin cape. . . ." The parallel to Kesey's
own costumed appearance at the Acid Test Graduation is obvious. After Quiston's drowning, Deboree's
egotism shifts to paranoia, and he begins to construct
an elaborate series of rationalizations. His eyes are
"shrewd" and his voice "petulant," and he is "smiling"
as he concludes: "I mean, you think I'm gonna pay for
this you got another think coming! It's just one of those
things . . . I'm a volunteer for Liberation of the
Universe and I don't care *how* many eggs get cracked.
I've got to be hard, you dig? Strong!" All the Animal
Friends are appalled, and even Behema is shown
"*biting her lip while tears stream at the sight of her
shrinking superman.*"

Then, surrealistically, the Animal Friends grow
in size, dwarfing Deboree as they "step out of their
parts . . . like a tired troupe of Thespians" and stand
revealed as gods. They proceed to debate Deboree's
fate, citing his "heedless press for power and
vengeance." They view him "like a zoo tour pausing
before an interesting specimen," yet they also see him
as "a promising tenderfoot." Although their council
comes close to voting for Abandonment, which they
recognize would leave Deboree irrevocably alone and
hopeless, their ultimate decision is a merciful Reversal.
This process is represented in explicitly cinematic terms:

ALL (standing): Let it run back . . . Back run it let. . . .
*They begin to slow down before Deboree's eyes, slowing
until the individual frames can be seen flickering by,
then stopping, then flickering into motion again in the
opposite direction, words and all, picking up speed
backwards. . . .*

The terrified Deboree, "wrenched about like an

agonized puppet," cries out humbly: "This isn't the me I wish, either! It's a weakness! a pride! a comicbook daydream but please believe *this isn't me*! . . . Help me . . . *change*! Oh God forgive me. . . . Let me try again to be, my God. . . ."

The backward flow of time stops. Quiston's cry for help is heard again, and this time Deboree promptly and courageously rescues him, taking his first step toward a new courage and humility. The following morning, a chastened and pensive Deboree begins his return trip to the United States with his family and friends. If he wonders which of the previous night's events really happened and which were LSD hallucinations, the reader need not, because "it's true even if it didn't happen."

Technically, the conclusion of "Over the Border" is reminiscent of both *Cuckoo's Nest* (particularly in the use of physical size as hallucinatory metaphor) and *Notion* (in the use of time as a flexible continuum). Deboree's crisis and subsequent moral development are parallel to those of several earlier characters: McMurphy, Lee Stamper, and particularly Hank. In the latter case, Joby's death by drowning prefigures Quiston's. But the most significant statement here, and the most crucial revelation in all of *Kesey's Garage Sale*, is Kesey's candid admission of the degree to which his own destructive egocentricity had grown in the 1960s. Kesey implicitly announces here a new maturity.

In *The Electric Kool-Aid Acid Test*, Wolfe showed Kesey's identification with comic-book superheroes.[3] More important, Wolfe pointed out Kesey's interest in the work of the German philosopher Friedrich Nietzsche and his concept of the *Ubermensch*, or Superman. This interest is reinforced by Deboree's recurrent allusions to Nietzsche's *Thus Spake Zarathustra* in "Over the Border." For example, Deboree, interrupted in his reading of *Zarathustra* by Undine, explains to her:

DEBOREE: . . . But if man has not become his ultimate
consciousness—if he is metamorphosing into the
Ubermensch. . . .

UNDINE: What's the *Ubermensch*?

DEBOREE: What all the Animal Friends and similar groups
are working to become: the Superman. We are all along
on this trip as apprentice supermen.

Clearly, this concept provides Deboree with part of
the rationalization for his vanity and pursuit of power.
Yet the conclusion of the screenplay, with its pointed
reference to Deboree as a "shrinking superman," suggests that Kesey ultimately rejected the more simplistic
and melodramatic manifestations of this pursuit.

The development of Kesey's conception of himself
and his place in the cosmic order is rendered
dramatically more clear through an autobiographical
anecdote that appears only a few pages after the conclusion of "Over the Border." He begins by telling how
the first drug trips freed him and his friends from the
old shells which had imprisoned them. But, he continues, the drugs themselves began to form the basis
for new shells. A new revelation was necessary: "But
something there is that doesn't love a wall. Another
round of treatments wasn't long in coming down.
Only this time the shocks went deeper. To the heart of
matters, so to speak." He goes on to tell of driving into
a collision with a train and of the apparent death and
resuscitation of his younger son, Jed:

He didn't look hurt anywhere but *Oh* he was such desolate
heaviness in my arms. . . . And he sighed, a curiously
familiar sigh . . . and I felt the life go out of him. . . . My
ear found no beating at his chest. . . . There I sat . . .
holding my dead son in my arms. . . . Then I closed my
eyes . . . and called aloud:
    "O dear Lord, please don't let him die." Then things
became completely calm . . . then I knew what to do. Opening my eyes I leaned back to Jed and began to give him mouth
to mouth resuscitation. . . . Finally Jed sighed again, the

same soft wings except this time they bore the life back into its sacred vessel.

I knew I had participated in a miracle and I was absolutely amazed. . . . That returning sigh will sound through all the rest of my life and I will be ever thankful. What amazed me, though, was that when the chips were down I knew *where* to call, and that I knew Who answered.

The first tool I would like to point out, then, is the Bible. All of it. All the rest of your life.

The situation and the revelation it brought are evocative of Deboree's experience at the conclusion of "Over the Border." In both the autobiographical account and the fictional vision it may have informed, it is difficult not to be impressed by Kesey's personal growth.

His growth as an artist is another matter. Ultimately, *Kesey's Garage Sale*, the virtues of "Over the Border" notwithstanding, cannot be seen as a major achievement in itself. Clearly, it is dwarfed by *Cuckoo's Nest* and *Notion*. But it provides further insight into those novels; and in Kesey's revelation here of his growing respect for the virtues of faith, humility, and patience can be found the basis for his forthcoming novel, *Seven Prayers*, and for its narrator-protagonist, Grandma Whittier.

6

Spit in the Ocean
and *Seven Prayers*
by Grandma Whittier:
"In the Shadow Land"

In their interview in *Kesey's Garage Sale*, Kesey told
Paul Krassner:

You are you from conception and that never changes no matter what physical changes your body takes. And the virile
sport in the Mustang driving to work with his muscular
forearm tanned and ready for a day's labor has *not one
microgram more* right to his inalienable rights of life, liberty
and the pursuit of happiness than has the three month's foetus
riding in a sack of water or the vegetable rotting for twenty
years in a gurney bed. Who's to know the value or extent of
another's trip? How can we assume that the world through
the windshield of that Mustang is any more rich or holy or
even sane than the world before those pale blue eyes?[1]

Kesey's belief in the value of all life and his concern
with the plight of the elderly in American society are
reflected in his magazine, *Spit in the Ocean* (SITO),
and even more in his novel in progress, *Seven Prayers
by Grandma Whittier*.

Five issues of *Spit in the Ocean* have been
published to date. The first, subtitled "Old in the
Streets," was organized around the theme of old age.
It was edited by Kesey and was published in 1974. The
second issue, guest edited by the pseudonymous "my,"
was published in 1976 and subtitled "Getting There

From Here!" The third issue (Fall 1977), edited by
Timothy Leary, dealt with "Communication with
Higher Intelligence." The fourth (Winter 1977),
"Straight from the Gut," was a feminist issue edited by
Lee Marrs. The fifth (Summer 1979), edited by
Richard and Elaine Loren, was entitled "The Pyramid
Issue" and consisted largely of a reprint of Kesey's
"Search for the Secret Pyramid." Issue six, "The
Cassady Issue," will be edited by Ken Babbs and
devoted entirely to the late, legendary Neal Cassady,
Kesey's most flamboyant bus trip companion.

What makes SITO worthy of more than a brief
mention is the fact that Kesey's new novel, *Seven
Prayers by Grandma Whittier*, is being serialized
through its seven-issue run. In the first two issues,
Kesey used the name of the novel's narrator-
protagonist as his pseudonym, and its title was simply
Seven Prayers. Gradually, what had never been a very
closely guarded secret emerged, and after hints and
then an open declaration of authorship, Kesey began
listing the episodes in the contents page of SITO as
"Ken Kesey: *Seven Prayers by Grandma Whittier*."
The segments published to date indicate that this is
the most substantial piece of writing Kesey has done
since 1964.

The structure of the work is episodic. On each of
seven nights, beginning with Good Friday, Rebecca
Topple (Grandma) Whittier prays for divine guidance
and then elaborates at length on the day's events. The
narrative is often stream-of-consciousness, usually
measured and precise in recreating situation and
dialogue. It is always credibly rendered in Grandma's
own language, informed by folk wisdom and a famili-
arity with the Bible, except for those passages in which
an omniscient third-person narrator takes over briefly.

On Good Friday, coincidentally her eighty-sixth
birthday, Grandma is picked up at her Eugene,
Oregon, high-rise apartment by her eldest grandson,

the "famous" Devlin Deboree, and taken to his dairy farm for a birthday celebration and gala "worship fair." He is accompanied by his black friend Montgomery Keller-Brown, sometimes known as M'kehla,[2] and the latter's four-year-old son October, nicknamed Toby, as well as a clownish actor and movie producer, Otis Kone. At the farm, Devlin's wife, Betsy, and children, Sherree, Quiston, and Caleb, and a host of guests await her. The bright and charming Toby is strikingly blue-eyed, and so Grandma tacitly assumes that M'kehla's wife is white. But Levity Keller-Brown turns out to be black; and this circumstance, coupled with Otis's arch references to her father's wealth and, implicitly, to her infidelity, makes Grandma acutely sensitive to M'kehla's smoldering anger. Despite her considerable tact and diplomacy, he turns on the old woman herself.

The remainder of the book to date focuses on the growing conflict between Keller-Brown and Grandma and on her hazard-fraught journey with her adopted companions, Toby and Otis, to escape him. Superficially charming, M'kehla soon reveals himself as cruel and vindictive, a malevolent creature described in occult terms. Concerned and curious about his relationship with his son, Grandma accepts his invitation to ride in his bus to Los Angeles and from there through the South to her original home state, Arkansas, ostensibly to conduct some personal business involving mineral rights. After several reversals of attitude, Grandma becomes sufficiently convinced of Keller-Brown's evil nature to flee with Toby and Otis; the unlikely trio travel first to Las Vegas by air and then into New Mexico by train, employing various disguises and all their ingenuity as M'kehla and the police follow one step behind.

This flight suggests certain parallels to William Faulkner's last novel, *The Reivers*, in which an unlikely trio made up of a black, a young boy, and a thick-headed bumbler appropriate a car and embark on a journey in which they encounter boisterous sin, evil adversaries, and a series of humorously improbable adventures. The novel is narrated in the first person by the young boy, now an old man, to his grandchildren. The primary difference between *Seven Prayers* and *The Reivers* is that the improbable and outrageous adventures of Grandma and company are more frightening than humorous. The world which Kesey posits is pervaded by malevolence.

Grandma's growing perception of the mystery surrounding Keller-Brown/M'kehla makes up much of the primary action of the novel's first segment, which establishes the characters of the major antagonists and the supernatural tone which informs the entire work. Although Keller-Brown is stately and proud in demeanor, utterly courtly and deferential at first in his treatment of Mrs. Whittier, disturbing inconsistencies soon begin to arise. Upon their first meeting, she describes him as

. . . tall, elegant, straightbacked and squareshouldered and features like the grains in a polished wood, a rare hardwood, from some far-off land. . . . Most of all, though, with a set to his deep dark eyes like I never saw on another earthly being. It wasn't just that he didn't blink; lawyers can look at you without blinking. But this fellow was looking at you all the way from the center of the earth! I found myself fiddling at my collarbuttons and mumbling howdy like a little girl.[3]

Despite his externally attractive appearance, his role as leader of a gospel singing group called the Birds of Prayer, and his extensive knowledge of the Bible, Keller-Brown soon begins to seem a representative of evil, one who might well "look at you from the center of the earth." Reclining in the back of his opulently customized bus during the trip to the worship fair, Grandma momentarily imagines him looking at her; and although his back is turned, "it seemed I felt sure enough a heavy dark look brush me, like an actual touch, Lord, like an actual physical presence" (SITO 1/117).

During the bus trip, Grandma gives Toby a white cameo necklace, which he tells his father came to him while he slept from "a *white* angel" (SITO 1/118), and later, Toby possessively adopts the sole remaining kitten of Devlin's Siamese cat. The two seemingly innocent gifts precipitate in M'kehla a terrifying rage. That night, Grandma discovers the kitten dead under a rock, with the necklace knotted around its neck. And as she walks alone toward her cabin in the bright moonlight,

. . . he was suddenly in front of me—a sharp black pyramid in the moonlight, those two eyes boring down at me, hissing: "Backdoor! Don't you never come slippin' in the backdoor on *my* little boy again, y'understand? *never!* That necklace I let pass 'cause I say 'She old. She just old. She don't know.' But then to pull the same bullshit about the motherfucking *cat* . . . that's backdoor." Two big hands from somebody behind grabbed both sides of my head . . . I couldn't holler or turn aside or even blink. "White angel, my ass! *I* show *you*, white angel!" It was like he pulled back the dark blouse of his face and two breasts come straining out towards me swirling and drooping out and down until the black nipples touched my very eyeballs . . . giving suck . . . milking into me such thoughts and pictures that my mind knew at once not to think about or look at (SITO 1/123-124).

Despite his air, carefully cultivated by exotic dress and accoutrements, of being "from some far-off land," Keller-Brown in his fury here lapses into a funky southern black dialect. Yet the frighteningly mystical terms in which Grandma perceives the confrontation suggest that he is, in a more profound sense, an alien being.

Rushing to her cabin, Grandma takes sleeping pills and eventually drifts into a dream-tormented sleep, from which she is awakened by the screams of Otis, who, apparently hallucinating, runs madly about the farm shouting in terror until subdued by his companions. It is later revealed that both Otis and Grandma have been dosed with hallucinogens by Keller-Brown. The segment ends as she prays to God for a sign to confirm what she thinks she has confronted.

This first prayer serves to establish Grandma's character clearly. Though horrified, she is not afraid for her own physical safety. She is rendered as a courageous, deeply religious woman without a trace of self-pity. In addition, she tells us at the outset of a mystical experience she had in childhood when, apparently dead from a fall, she felt her soul leave her body, only to be turned back at the gates of heaven by an angel, who told her that she was predestined to serve a full century of life on earth and to become a saint. Therefore, Grandma emphasizes in her prayer that

I am not shivering scared here on my knees like some dried-up old time miser pinchin life like her last measly pennies. . . . What I'm asking for is I guess a sign of some kind. . . . What I'm afraid of I can't put a name to yet, having just this day encountered it like finding a new-hatched freak of nature, but it is not of dying. Moreover I am not even sure whether my fear is of a real McCoy danger or not. Is this dirty business I think I perceive really occurring? (SITO 1/105)

The ambiguity articulated by Grandma is soon resolved by further duplicity on the part of Keller-Brown, precipitating her flight with Toby and Otis.

Although it is incomplete, certain structural, thematic, and symbolic patterns begin to emerge at this stage of the novel's development. As Grandma and her motley crew move across the country toward her childhood home, the journey motif provides an obvious structural bulwark for the plot. But the primary structural device upon which Kesey relies is clearly the series of first-person, italicized prayers themselves, which open each section of the novel. Not only do these touch, often suspensefully, upon the salient events of the day just past, piquing the reader's interest, they incorporate lengthy digressions from Grandma's past experience, providing extensive exposition and character development and helping to make Grandma Whittier a credible narrator and sympathetic protagonist. As each day's adventures are digested, she draws parallels to experiences of her childhood or young adulthood, and the anecdotes thus related are almost invariably integral to understanding Grandma's present situation and her reactions to it.

Thus, many absent or dead family members are introduced to the reader through Grandma's reminiscences: her deceased husband, Emerson Thoreau Whittier (with a grandfather named after three American writers, it is no surprise that Devlin Deboree became one himself), her parents, and her children.

Most central, however, is her uncle, Richard "Dicker" Topple, who emerges throughout the novel as a recurrent touchstone for honesty, shrewdness, and wisdom. Long dead, Uncle Dicker remains nonetheless a pervasive mentor in Grandma's consciousness. For instance, his example in exposing a card sharp, whose ingenious ploy involved using salt secreted in his unlighted cigar to mark invisibly the card which his blind confederate then identified, directly influences Grandma's understanding of M'kehla's use of salt to mark the Bible page he wishes Toby to read "randomly" to an audience. Past experience directly influences present action when Grandma tells Toby the story of Uncle Dicker and the salted cards, implicitly giving him the moral guidance to renounce his own role in the salted Bible confidence game. The conversation is overheard by Larry the Lugger, a sly flunky who confronts M'kehla with it for his own gain and is consequently killed in a freeway "accident" after Keller-Brown doses him with the powerful hallucinogen STP. Further repercussions are clearly in store for Grandma and for Toby, whose physical safety and moral salvation concern her more than her own.

Toby is clearly an attractive and sympathetic character whose intelligence and intuitive perception of adult hypocrisy do not obviate his very real innocence. The secret of his paternity is an intriguing mystery, highlighting his importance as a central figure in the novel's primary conflict: between Grandma and Keller-Brown and between the religious values each represents.

As Toby has explained to Grandma, his future has been planned already by his father. He is to be the preacher of a united worldwide congregation in a future era when nations no longer exist. The prospect seems an attractive if unrealistic one to her while she is still unsure of Keller-Brown's alliance with good or evil, and she admits that "it would take more than just an ordinary power not to follow him" (SITO 2/149). But once this uncertainty is resolved in her mind by the revelation of the father's manipulative use of his son to hoodwink audiences, the future prediction appears an insidious scheme. The salvation of Toby's innocence from his father's machinations becomes, as Grandma perceives it, her God-given mission:

From the instant I had come across that telltale salt in my Bible I had been convinced the Lord intended me to someway take the rod in hand and switch the little fellow out of the valley of shadow and shilly shally that his father was leading him down, and set his little feet on the path of Righteousness. The problem was how (SITO 3/136).

The "how" involves flight and, though Toby eagerly accompanies Grandma, an ostensible kidnaping.

A primary theme in *Seven Prayers* (as in *Cuckoo's Nest* and *Notion*) is the irony of external appearance as opposed to inner reality. Thus, Montgomery Keller-Brown appears courtly, dignified, and virtuous, an appearance which belies his cruel and vindictive nature. Otis Kone, apparently a buffoon of no redeeming virtues, gradually reveals certain attractive qualities—loyalty, resourcefulness, and personal vulnerability—while remaining an essentially comic figure. Most important, Grandma Whittier's great virtues—courage, humility, compassion, and intelligence—are masked by her outwardly unattractive physical appearance. She is "old as night" (SITO 3/117), and one side of her face has been disfigured since the girlhood accident that sent her to heaven and back. Ironically, it is Keller-Brown who upon their first meeting calls Grandma "an obviously beautiful soul" (SITO 1/113), a judgment which the reader shares throughout.

During their flight, the fugitives are followed across the country by ubiquitous television news broadcasts in which Grandma is portrayed as a vicious kidnapper, and the characterization is graphically supported by a freeze frame of her scarred face. As we all know from experience, the camera often *does* lie when one frozen moment is represented as the total truth. Furthermore, the negative role of television as a distorter of truth and a purveyor of artificiality is a recurrent one in the novel. Nonetheless, Grandma is forced to admit sadly at the conclusion of Prayer Four that she has "become a monster in the eyes of the world" (SITO 4/140). Elaborating on this thought, she draws a sardonic allusion to the pursuit of the monster in the various movie versions of *Frankenstein*: "All them viewers lacked was pitchforks and torches."

The confusion caused by external appearance is exacerbated by the disguises affected by the fugitives. Otis, his clothing stolen, appears in an old theatrical costume as a leprechaun, and the cheap green dye causes his skin to turn green. Later, he wears a sailor suit, masquerades as a Gold Star mother, and with the aid of shoe polish becomes a Hindu guru. Grandma sardonically summarizes her own external metamorphoses in Prayer Five: "Day before yesterday I was a old white angel and yesterday I was a black grand-

mammy and all day today I been the mysterious . . .
Hindoo Indian . . . so tonight I might's well be a
squaw from Santa Fe" (SITO 5/144).

In changing the color of her skin and temporarily
joining various minority groups, Grandma is exposed
to racial prejudice, notably in the USO lounge of an
airport. Although she has always repudiated this most
extreme of external judgments, the firsthand experience adds to her compassion. While both Grandma
and Otis actually change color, Toby does not. Instead, he is given the opportunity to reject the stylized
religious robes affected by his father and to melt into a
precious childhood anonymity he has never before
known, in jeans, T-shirt, and sunglasses. Proudly, he
becomes a prowling "tomcat" (SITO 5/165). In fact,
he is so anxious to rid himself of the regal purple shoes
which are the last vestige of his religious costume that
he slips into his father's parked bus to change to his
sneakers, and the abandoned purple shoes put Keller-
Brown back on the trail.

Purple, with its connotations of regal or biblical
opulence, is a color favored by Keller-Brown. On his
white bus, five purple birds flying in a cross formation
are the symbol of his singing group, the Birds of
Prayer, a name which in its pun on "birds of prey" suggests the duality of M'kehla, the pious exterior masking
the predator within. Other horrible, half-human
were-creatures, many of them birds, appear as the
novel progresses. On the first night, sleeping fitfully
under the hallucinogen with which Keller-Brown has
dosed her, Grandma dreams of a malevolent "shadow
thing—sometimes it was an alligator, sometimes it was
a panther or a wolf" (SITO 1/124). The evil figures
take clearer shape later. If, as Grandma suggests,
Keller-Brown is "a hound of hell" (SITO 5/143),
various attendant creatures appear to hinder her
escape from him. On the airplane to Las Vegas, the
stewardess is "some girl-thing in a polyester

uniform . . . some kind of pretty witch, all teeth and eyes and about to eat us all" (SITO 5/145). On the ground, the fugitive trio are confronted by an unsympathetic ticket agent, presented in an extended metaphor as a were-owl, with "beak" and "talons" (SITO 5/147), "like something that was made to look like a human, but was really a predatory spirit in disguise. . . . Maybe Satan sent . . . maybe just a owl trying to pass" (SITO 5/149).

Next is an albino "crane" of a motel clerk, and the next morning a lizard-woman, "another thing ugly with an even uglier evil inside of it" (SITO 5/165), from which Grandma rescues Toby. Finally, just before the escape from Las Vegas, Grandma encounters, in a club called The Gilded Cage, a cocktail waitress named Cockatoo who is dressed like a bird, touches her with "a hand, cold as the beak of a buzzard," and offers her a drink called a "Rooster Tail" (SITO 5/169). The mechanical creatures of technology, too, are perceived as monsters, such as the airliner "painted a fleshy fuchsia obscene *pink*" (SITO 3/122), with a grinning face painted on its front, and the huge television camera at the Hollywood Bowl, "big as a holy dinosaur, people at its feet tending its every need. I mean a very *church* of a monster" (SITO 4/120).

The richness of extended metaphor and the intense subjectivity throughout these descriptions are reminiscent of Bromden's perceptions of the world of the Combine. Like Bromden, Grandma has an intuitive awareness of the falsity and evil lying beneath the surface of society. In fact, in an observation similar to "It's true even if it didn't happen," Grandma tells us that "In the shadow land the hawks are just as dangerous dreamed as actual" (SITO 5/142). But unlike Bromden, Grandma never hides from responsibility in a fog, nor is her sanity or courage ever in doubt. And her clarity and quickness of mind are among her primary assets throughout the novel. As her name suggests, she outwits her adversaries because she is "wittier."

There are pitfalls enough in evaluating the work of a living author without compounding them by making absolute judgments on a work in progress. The truncated state of the fragment under discussion is both exciting and frustrating. The outcome of Grandma Whittier's adventures is still unknown, as are such intentional mysteries and ambiguities as the identity of Toby's biological father and the ultimate role of M'kehla. What is clear is that Kesey has completed most of a substantial third novel which should be published in book form in the relatively near future.

If *Seven Prayers* does not appear at present to rival the complexity and force of Kesey's first two novels, it is nonetheless part of the continuum of his work, growing obviously out of his technical and thematic preoccupations. Like *Cuckoo's Nest*, *Seven Prayers* relies primarily on a highly subjective first-person narrative in which the perception of evil is reflected in bizarre ways and the relation between external appearance and internal reality is explored. As in *Sometimes a Great Notion*, Kesey uses the journey motif, an interweaving of past and present, and shifts from first- to third-person point of view, although these devices are not as intricately developed here. *Seven Prayers* is a decidedly simpler and less ambitious novel than either *Notion* or *Cuckoo's Nest*. Yet it is evidence that Kesey's last word has not yet been heard.

7

Conclusion: The Pinnacle of Kesey's Art

In *Garage Sale*, Kesey touches humorously and self-deprecatingly on the issue of his public image:

Well, I *do* think about my fucking image, I confess. I don't intend to but often I find it there in the hallway, prancing and whimpering like a dog begging to be taken for a walk in the park, and I am compelled, out of kindness if nothing else, to deal with it.

As suggested at the outset of this study, Kesey's public image does influence the reception of his work. That image, and frequent critical oversimplifications of *Cuckoo's Nest*, have led to such feminist judgments of Kesey as the one by Robin Morgan which he quotes good-naturedly in *Garage Sale*: "To be a real Ken Kesey-type man, one should slap dumb women, and shoot dumb animals, and in the true Hemingway mystique, God forbid, not be a FAG."[1] Kesey's response to Morgan's lecture, at which he was present, was that "There wasn't one of us watching that didn't know down under our pricked pride that the freedoms Ms. Morgan was frightening us with were as much to man's benefit as to woman's."

Despite Kesey's public statements, here and elsewhere, in favor of women's liberation, the rigid preconception of him as a misogynist still recurs, often linked with the accusation of racism. For example, in a lengthy letter to *The New York Times*, reprinted in

John C. Pratt's Viking Critical Library edition of *One
Flew Over the Cuckoo's Nest*, Marcia L. Falk attacks
both the play and novel versions of *Cuckoo's Nest* as
"blatant sexism" and goes on to state that "Nurse
Ratched is a woman because Ken Kesey hates and
fears women," concluding with a repudiation of the
"psychic disease out of which the book's vision was
born."[2] She accuses Kesey of perpetuating sexist and
racist stereotypes and, blinded by her rage, lapses frequently into such jargon-ridden statements as:

Somehow, in the confused vision of the author and
playwright, the refusal of women, an oppressed class, to utterly submit to male-oriented social structures is identified
with the attack of white men, the oppressor class, on peoples
of color.[3]

Falk's doctrinaire oversimplifications are so
patently narrow in vision that it would seem un-
necessary to defend Kesey and his work against them.
Yet apparently, enough people hold similar views to
prompt Janet R. Sutherland to write "A Defense of
Ken Kesey's *One Flew Over the Cuckoo's Nest*,"[4] in
which she feels compelled to explain that the book con-
demns rather than espouses such values as racism.

Unfortunately, much of the criticism of *Cuckoo's
Nest* published to date comprises attacks on and
defenses of the perceived values of the novel and its
author and their literary worth. Thus, when Terence
Martin published a positive critical assessment of the
novel in *Modern Fiction Studies*,[5] it was answered in
the same journal by Robert Forrey, who described
Cuckoo's Nest as "conservative, if not reactionary,
politically; sexist, if not psychopathological,
psychologically; and very low, if not downright
lowbrow, in terms of the level of sensibility it
reflects."[6] Forrey went on to make pejorative reference
to the "repressed homosexuality that seems to pervade
it"[7] and concluded that "those who think *One Flew*

Over the Cuckoo's Nest one of the great novels of our
time and McMurphy an indomitable culture hero . . .
have been . . . gulled."[8]

In addition to these accusations, Kesey's first
novel has been denigrated as a simplistic vision of life,
no more subtle than a comic book. Thus, Terry G.
Sherwood, in *"One Flew Over the Cuckoo's Nest* and
the Comic Strip," after a fairly balanced treatment of
the novel, concludes that:

Kesey believes in the comic strip world in spite of himself.
This is the moral ground on which critical faultfinding must
begin. Kesey has not avoided the dangers of a simplistic
aesthetic despite his attempts to complicate it. He forgets that
the comic strip world is not an answer to life, but an escape
from it.[9]

And Leslie Fiedler feels that "One might, indeed, have
imagined Kesey ending up as a comic book writer, but
since the false second start of *Sometimes a Great Notion*, he has preferred to live his comic strip rather
than write or even draw it."[10]

These are, of course, not the only critical directions that have been taken. There are also intelligent
articles, book chapters, and dissertations, such as those
by Stephen L. Tanner,[11] Tony Tanner,[12] Raymond
Olderman,[13] and Ronald G. Billingsley,[14] which emphasize the subtlety, power, and literary value of
Kesey's work.

As I believe I have shown in my critical treatment, *One Flew Over the Cuckoo's Nest* is both complex in technique and humanistic in vision. But even
those who subscribe to the pejorative critical
judgments of this novel as sexist, racist, or simplistic
would have a good deal more trouble defending those
judgments in light of Kesey's later writings. First,
there are the strong and admirable figure of Viv, the
fair and balanced treatments of Hank's adversaries,
the massive and intricate structure of *Sometimes a*

Great Notion. Then, in *Kesey's Garage Sale* and *Spit in the Ocean*, there are Kesey's forthright statements in favor of women's rights and those of all people of whatever age or race, and his renunciation in "Over the Border" of his own destructive egocentricity. Finally, there is the palpable irony that Kesey's protagonist in *Seven Prayers by Grandma Whittier* is an old woman and that her companions are a black child and a white male who is far from the "macho" image reviled by many feminist critics.

Unfortunately, the vast preponderance of Kesey criticism has limited itself to *Cuckoo's Nest*. It is understandable that little critical attention has been paid to *Kesey's Garage Sale* or *Seven Prayers*, but the relative neglect of *Sometimes a Great Notion* by most critics is indefensible. It is not, however, inexplicable. *Notion* is a difficult novel to read. Ronald Billingsley goes so far as to state in the lengthy and generally intelligent exegesis he accords it in his dissertation that it can be understood properly only after a second reading. Thus, for every incisive treatment of what Kesey has done in *Notion*, such as that of Tony Tanner in *City of Words*, there are numerous critics who ignore the novel or, worse, dismiss it as "awkwardly prolix"[15] or as a "*strained* effort—for all its occasional successes somehow an error."[16]

These reactions to *Sometimes a Great Notion* are incomprehensible to me. I find myself in a literary situation analogous to that of Joan Didion when she reviewed *The Executioner's Song*, Norman Mailer's massive book about the life and death of Gary Gilmore. She wrote angrily:

It is one of those testimonies to the tenacity of self-regard in the literary life that large numbers of people remain persuaded that Norman Mailer is no better than their reading of him. They condescend to him, they dismiss his most original work in favor of the more literal and predictable rhythms of *The Armies of the Night*; they regard *The Naked and the*

Dead as a promise later broken and every book since as . . . a stalling action . . . for the "big book" he cannot write.[17]

I feel similarly about Kesey's performance in *Sometimes a Great Notion*. It is unquestionably his masterpiece.

Yet the inescapable question arises of why Kesey has written so little fiction since *Notion*. Although the phenomenon is not an uncommon one among American novelists—Hemingway, Fitzgerald, and Mailer, for example, each had a lapse of almost a decade between novels at about the same age—Kesey's production until recently has been exceptionally small. One answer may lie in this exchange from the Krassner interview:

Q. Didn't you once believe that writing is an old-fashioned and artificial occupation?
A. I was counting on the millennium. Now I guess I'm tired of waiting.

In the years after the publication of *Sometimes a Great Notion*, Kesey became impatient with the limitations of the printed page as a medium of communication. In his search for more immediate, even instantaneous communication (as in the Acid Tests), he steeped himself in a complex tangle of human relationships and escalating drug use which, combined with the consequent personal and legal problems, were hardly conducive to disciplined writing.

Realizing that he had taken the wrong direction, Kesey moved back toward writing; yet his output remains painfully slow, perhaps because of other preoccupations in his life. As he remarked in a more recent interview:

My family is ten times more important to me than my writing. I don't do too much writing at home because of the stench I stir up. . . . I used to write as if the world was coming to an end but it no longer concerns me. I write as if the world will go on.[18]

The fact seems to be that in achieving a greater personal equanimity and maturity, Kesey has lost the sense of urgency in his writing commitment. If this frustrates his most loyal readers, we must remind ourselves of how fortunate we have been to get what we have.

It is customary to make disclaimers when venturing judgments about the future work of a living author, but in the case of Kesey it is doubtful whether subsequent novels, be they few or many, will make a substantial difference in the literary value of his work. Another literary analogy may be in order here. If Ernest Hemingway had died at the age of thirty-five, we would have had a good deal less of his work, but we would have had his best: *The Sun Also Rises*, *A Farewell to Arms*, and many of the finest short stories.

Kesey's situation is similar. Whether he leaves behind at the close of his career three novels or ten, we have already had his best. *Sometimes a Great Notion* is the work upon which his literary reputation will ultimately rest; for it is in this magnificent, powerful novel that we see Ken Kesey at the pinnacle of his art.

Notes

1. Biography

1. Tom Wolfe, *The Electric Kool-Aid Acid Test* (New York: Bantam Books, Inc., 1969). For much of the factual material about Kesey's life through 1967, I am indebted to this book.
2. The novel is dedicated "To Vik Lovell / who told me dragons did not exist, / then led me to their lairs."
3. Wolfe, *Acid Test*, pp. 42–43.
4. Tony Tanner, *City of Words: American Fiction 1950–1970*, (New York: Harper & Row, 1971), p. 390.
5. Wolfe, *Acid Test*, p. 91.
6. Robert Scholes, "Double Perspective on Hysteria," *Saturday Review*, August 24, 1968, p. 37.
7. Wolfe, *Acid Test*, p. 35.
8. Ibid., p. 69.
9. Ibid., p. 82.
10. Ibid., p. 83.
11. Ibid., p. 352.
12. Ibid., p. 159.
13. Ibid., pp. 172–173.
14. Ibid., p. 175.
15. Norman Mailer, *Advertisements for Myself* (New York: G. P. Putnam's Sons, 1959), p. 234.
16. Wolfe, *Acid Test*, p. 235.
17. Ibid., p. 272.
18. Ibid., p. 327.
19. Kesey sued and ultimately settled for 2.5% of the movie's net, which was expected to give him an eventual total of $750,000 to $900,000, according to *Newsweek*, January 10, 1977, p. 13.

20.   John Riley, "Bio: Novelist Ken Kesey Has Flown the
      'Cuckoo's Nest' and Given Up Tripping for Farming,"
      People Weekly, March 22, 1976, p. 26.

        2.   *One Flew Over the Cuckoo's Nest*

1.   Other obvious structural analogies are suggested by
      Robert Penn Warren's *All the King's Men* and Norman
      Mailer's *The Deer Park*.
2.   The existential aspects of the choice to define oneself
      will be dealt with in the chapter on *Sometimes a Great
      Notion*, in which they are central to Kesey's thematic
      statement.
3.   In American folklore, black aces and eights are known
      as the "dead man's hand" because this was the poker
      hand held by Wild Bill Hickok when he was shot
      to death.

        3.   Stage and Screen Adaptations

1.   John Riley, "Bio: Novelist Ken Kesey Has Flown the
      'Cuckoo's Nest' and Given Up Tripping for Farming,"
      People Weekly, March 22, 1976, p. 25.
2.   Ibid.
3.   Jack Kroll, "You're All Right, Jack," *Newsweek*,
      November 24, 1975, p. 113.
4.   Dale Wasserman, *One Flew Over the Cuckoo's Nest: A
      Play in Two Acts from the Novel by Ken Kesey* (New
      York: Samuel French, Inc., 1970), p. 6.
5.   Kroll, p. 113.
6.   Wasserman, p. 58.

        4.   *Sometimes a Great Notion*

1.   Ken Kesey, "Letter to Ken Babbs: ['Peyote and Point of
      View']," in Ken Kesey, *One Flew Over the Cuckoo's
      Nest: Text and Criticism*, ed. John C. Pratt, Viking
      Critical Library (New York: Viking Press, 1973), p. 338.

2. In terms of their subjectivity, these passages are reminis-
    cent of John Dos Passos's use of *The Camera Eye* in his
    USA trilogy.
3. Tony Tanner, *City of Words*, p. 379.
4. The manner and motive of Willard's death are reminis-
    cent of Willy Loman's in Arthur Miller's *Death of a
    Salesman*, a parallel underlined by the similarity of the
    two characters' names.
5. From the song "Good Night, Irene," by Huddie Ledbet-
    ter and John Lomax.
6. This persistent use of hands as a primary symbol in both
    of Kesey's novels suggests several literary analogies.
    Among these are the development of Homer Simpson in
    Nathanael West's *The Day of the Locust*, Wing Bid-
    dlebaum in Sherwood Anderson's *Winesburg, Ohio*,
    and Mr. Antolini in J. D. Salinger's *The Catcher in the
    Rye*. In each of these characters, the symbolic value of
    the hands is largely devoted to the expression of sexual
    repression or ambivalence, a focus which is echoed
    throughout *Cuckoo's Nest* and, in *Notion*, concentrated
    primarily on Lee. As his soft hands become callused, he
    grows more confident in his ability to overcome his sex-
    ual impotence and ultimately to renounce his cowardice.
7. This perception of nature's indifference is as clearly
    naturalistic as that of Stephen Crane's Correspondent in
    "The Open Boat."
8. Paul Krassner, "An Impolite Interview with Ken
    Kesey," in Ken Kesey, *Kesey's Garage Sale*, (New York:
    Viking Press, 1973), p. 218.

5. *Kesey's Garage Sale*

1. The fact that the characters are easily identifiable with
    their counterparts among Kesey's family and friends is
    acknowledged by Kesey in the credits: ". . . with
    special thanks and apologies to the real lives and the
    true light that cast these shadows."
2. Ken Kesey, "The Day After Superman Died," *Esquire*
    92, no. 4 (October 1979), pp. 42–64.
3. Wolfe also points out Kesey's similarities to the
    charismatic protagonists of such novels as Robert

Heinlein's *Stranger in a Strange Land* and Hermann Hesse's *The Journey to the East.*

6. *Spit in the Ocean* and *Seven Prayers by Grandma Whittier*

1. Kesey goes on to denounce abortion as well as euthanasia. The fervor of his moral position makes one wonder whether he would now have any qualms about Bromden's mercy killing of McMurphy.
2. A character named "M'kehla" appears briefly in "Over the Border." Other recurrent characters among Devlin Deboree's circle of friends include Claude and Blanche Muddle.
3. Ken Kesey, *Seven Prayers by Grandma Whittier*, in *Spit in the Ocean*, no. 1 (1974), p. 113. Subsequent references to *Seven Prayers* will be documented parenthetically after each quotation, with both issue and page number (e.g., SITO 1/113). Full bibliographic data are given in the Bibliography.

7. Conclusion

1. Robin Morgan, quoted by Ken Kesey in *Kesey's Garage Sale*, p. 189.
2. Marcia L. Falk, "Letter to the Editor of *The New York Times*," in Ken Kesey, *One Flew Over the Cuckoo's Nest: Text and Criticism*, ed. John C. Pratt, Viking Critical Library (New York: Viking Press, 1973), p. 453.
3. Ibid., p. 451.
4. Janet R. Sutherland, "A Defense of Ken Kesey's *One Flew Over the Cuckoo's Nest*," *English Journal* 61 (January 1972), pp. 28–31.
5. Terence Martin, "*One Flew Over the Cuckoo's Nest* and the High Cost of Living," *Modern Fiction Studies* 19 (Spring 1973), pp. 43–55.
6. Robert Forrey, "Ken Kesey's Psychopathic Savior: A Rejoinder," *Modern Fiction Studies* 21 (Summer 1975), p. 222.

7. Ibid., p. 229.

8. Ibid., p. 230.

9. Terry G. Sherwood, "*One Flew Over the Cuckoo's Nest* and the Comic Strip," in Pratt, p. 396.

10. Leslie A. Fiedler, "The Higher Sentimentality," in Pratt, p. 378.

11. Stephen L. Tanner, "Salvation Through Laughter: Ken Kesey and the Cuckoo's Nest," *Southwest Review* 58 (Spring 1973), pp. 125–137.

12. Tony Tanner, *City of Words*, pp. 372–392.

13. Raymond Olderman, *Beyond the Waste Land: The American Novel in the Nineteen-Sixties*, (New Haven: Yale University Press, 1972), pp. 35–51.

14. Ronald G. Billingsley, "The Artistry of Ken Kesey" (Ph.D. diss., University of Oregon, 1971).

15. Kingsley Widmer, "The Post-Modernist Art of Protest: Kesey and Mailer as Expressions of Rebellion," *Centennial Review* 19, no. 3 (Summer 1975), p. 124.

16. Fiedler, in Pratt p. 378.

17. Joan Didion, review of *The Executioner's Song* by Norman Mailer, *New York Times Book Review*, October 7, 1979, p. 1.

18. Mamta Chaudhry-Fryer, "Ken Kesey: Sometimes a Great Writer," *The Prosery* 1 (Winter 1980), p. 39.

Bibliography

1. WORKS BY KEN KESEY

One Flew Over the Cuckoo's Nest. New York: Viking, 1962.
Sometimes a Great Notion. New York: Viking, 1964.
Kesey's Garage Sale. New York: Viking, 1973.
Seven Prayers by Grandma Whittier. Serialized in *Spit in the Ocean*, no. 1 (1974), pp. 102–127; no. 2 (Spring 1976), pp. 113–154; no. 3 (Fall 1977), pp. 113–141; no. 4 (Winter 1977), pp. 117–140; no. 5 (Summer 1979), pp. 135–176.

Stage Adaptation

Wasserman, Dale. *One Flew Over the Cuckoo's Nest: A Play in Two Acts from the Novel by Ken Kesey*. New York: Samuel French, Inc., 1970.

2. WORKS ABOUT KEN KESEY

Billingsley, Ronald Gregg. "The Artistry of Ken Kesey." Ph.D. dissertation, University of Oregon, 1971.

Carnes, Bruce. *Ken Kesey*. Boise: Boise State University Western Writers Series, Pamphlet No. 12, 1974.

Chaudhry-Fryer, Mamta. "Ken Kesey: Sometimes a Great Writer." *The Prosery* 1 (Winter 1980), pp. 34–39.

Fiedler, Leslie A. *The Return of the Vanishing American*. New York: Stein & Day, 1968.

Foster, J. W. "Hustling to Some Purpose: Kesey's *One Flew Over the Cuckoo's Nest*." *Western American Literature* 9 (August 1974), pp. 115–130.

Forrey, Robert. "Ken Kesey's Psychopathic Savior: A Rejoinder." *Modern Fiction Studies* 21 (Summer 1975), pp. 222–230.

Hill, Richard Allen. "The Law of Ken Kesey." Ph.D. dissertation, Emory University, 1976.

Huffman, James R. "The Cuckoo Clocks in Kesey's Nest." *Modern Language Studies* 7 (Spring 1977), pp. 62–73.

Kesey, Ken. *One Flew Over the Cuckoo's Nest: Text and Criticism.* Edited by John C. Pratt. Viking Critical Library, No. 9. New York: Viking, 1973.

Kroll, Jack. "You're All Right, Jack." *Newsweek*, November 24, 1975, p. 113.

Leeds, Barry H. "Theme and Technique in *One Flew Over the Cuckoo's Nest.*" *Connecticut Review* 7 (April 1974), pp. 35–50.

Lewis, Grover. "Who's the Bull Goose Loony Here?" *Playboy*, December 1975, p. 123.

Martin, Terence. "*One Flew Over the Cuckoo's Nest* and the High Cost of Living." *Modern Fiction Studies* 19 (Spring 1973), pp. 43–55.

McCreadie, Marsha. "*One Flew Over the Cuckoo's Nest:* Some Reasons for One Happy Adaptation." *Film Literature Quarterly* 5 (Spring 1977), pp. 125–131.

Mills, Nicolaus. "Ken Kesey and the Politics of Laughter." *Centennial Review* 16 (Winter 1972), pp. 41–61.

Olderman, Raymond. *Beyond the Waste Land: The American Novel in the Nineteen-Sixties.* New Haven: Yale University Press, 1972.

Riley, John. "Bio: Novelist Ken Kesey Has Flown the 'Cuckoo's Nest' and Given Up Tripping for Farming." *People Weekly*, March 22, 1976, pp. 25–28.

Safer, Elaine B. " 'It's the Truth Even If It Didn't Happen': Ken Kesey's *One Flew Over the Cuckoo's Nest.*" *Film Literature Quarterly* 5 (Spring 1977), pp. 132–141.

Scholes, Robert. "Double Perspective on Hysteria." *Saturday Review*, August 24, 1968, p. 37.

Sherman, W. D. "The Novels of Ken Kesey." *Journal of American Studies* 5 (August 1971), pp. 185–196.

Strelow, Michael et al., ed. *Kesey.* Eugene, Oregon: Northwest Review Books, 1977.

Sutherland, Janet R. "A Defense of Ken Kesey's *One Flew Over the Cuckoo's Nest.*" *English Journal* 61 (January 1972), pp. 28–31.

Tanner, Stephen L. "Salvation Through Laughter: Ken Kesey and the Cuckoo's Nest." *Southwest Review* 58 (Spring 1973), pp. 125–137.

Tanner, Tony. *City of Words: American Fiction 1950–1970.*
    New York: Harper & Row, 1971.
Tunnell, J. R. "Kesey and Vonnegut: Preachers of Redemp-
    tion." *Christian Century* 89 (1972), pp. 1180–1183.
Widmer, Kingsley. "The Post-Modernist Art of Protest: Kesey
    and Mailer as Expressions of Rebellion." *Centennial
    Review* 19 (Summer 1975), pp. 121–135.
Wolfe, Tom. *The Electric Kool-Aid Acid Test.* New York:
    Farrar, Straus and Giroux, 1968.
Zashin, Elliot M. "Political Theorist and Demiurge: The Rise
    and Fall of Ken Kesey." *Centennial Review* 17 (Spring
    1973), pp. 199–213.

Index

MODERN LITERATURE SERIES

In the same series (continued from page ii)